Anonymous

Poems of the Inner Life

Edition 6

Anonymous

Poems of the Inner Life
Edition 6

ISBN/EAN: 9783744717571

Printed in Europe, USA, Canada, Australia, Japan

Cover: Foto ©Thomas Meinert / pixelio.de

More available books at **www.hansebooks.com**

POEMS

OF

THE INNER LIFE.

SELECTED

CHIEFLY FROM MODERN AUTHORS

SIXTH EDITION.

LONDON :

SAMPSON LOW, MARSTON, SEARLE, & RIVINGTON,

CROWN BUILDINGS, 188, FLEET STREET.

1886.

PREFACE.

———◆———

A GLANCE at the Contents of this volume, and at the list of Authors from whose works the poems which it contains have been selected, will, perhaps, sufficiently show its general character and purpose.

It is a collection, not of sacred poetry, in the usual, technical sense of the term, but of poems which, without being ecclesiastical or theological, may be called religious, in so far as they have power to strengthen religious faith or to deepen religious impressions, and to express or suggest the spiritual significance of Nature and of Human Life. They have been selected according to a sense of what most nearly touches the heart and mind in our best and most earnest hours; and they reflect many moods of the soul, from that of questioning, and longing, and vague pathetic sadness, to the clear assurance of faith, and the peace and joy of communion with God.

Nothing has been chosen which has not seemed to have the mark of sincerity, and to show a real power of spiritual insight or feeling; and the selection has been tried by as high a standard of literary excellence as was practicable.

The difficulty, as may be supposed, has been, not to find materials for such a work, but to know how to select from the rich stores that were open to choose from. Those poems have, for the most part, been omitted which are contained in the numerous hymn-books and other familiar collections of sacred verse; while a special pleasure has been taken in calling the reader's attention to many less-known poems, which are not unworthy to have a place side by side with those which every lover of high and noble poetry has long known and delighted in.

In the plan and arrangement of the book nothing like an accurate classification of subjects has been attempted; but a few general divisions have been adopted, which may serve so to group the poems as to avoid any manifest incongruity in the order in which they stand.

In all cases the original text has been adhered to,

whenever it could be procured; and the very few omissions which have been made will be found mentioned in the notes at the end of the volume.

I beg to thank most sincerely the authors, publishers, and other owners of copyright, both English and American, who have so kindly and willingly given me permission to reprint the poems which I had selected.

R. C. J.

CONTENTS.

BOOK FIRST.—NATURE.

GIFTS.

		PAGE
The Inner Vision	*Wordsworth*	3
The Glory of Nature	*F. Tennyson*	4
The Lattice at Sunrise	*C. Turner*	5
The Forest Glade	*C. Turner*	6
May Carols	*Aubrey de Vere*	6
The Daffodils	*Wordsworth*	8
Eventide	*T. Burbidge*	9
Man	*George Herbert*	11
In Early Spring	*Wordsworth*	13
Each and All	*R. W. Emerson*	14
The Rainbow	*Wordsworth*	16
An Evening Voluntary	*Wordsworth*	16
The Last Day of Autumn	*From the German*	19
By the Sea	*Wordsworth*	20
Lines—Tintern Abbey	*Wordsworth*	21

LESSONS.

The Book of the World	*W. Drummond*	27
Love of Nature	*Wordsworth*	28
Insight	*J. R. Lowell*	28
Lessons from the Gorse	*E. B. Browning*	29
My Doves	*E. B. Browning*	30
To a Waterfowl	*W. C. Bryant*	33
The Redbreast in September	*J. Keble*	35

CONTENTS.

		PAGE
The Nightingale	*J. Keble*	36
Composed during a Storm	*Wordsworth*	39
The Constellation of the Plough	*Aubrey de Vere*	39
Quiet Work	*Matthew Arnold*	40

SYMBOLS.

To a Skylark	*Wordsworth*	41
The Sound of the Sea	*H. W. Longfellow*	42
The Trosachs	*Wordsworth*	42
A May Carol	*Aubrey de Vere*	43
The Skylark	*F. Tennyson*	44
Flower and Fruit	*F. Tennyson*	46
The Honeysuckle	*Dante G. Rossetti*	48
Symbols	*Christina Rossetti*	49
Æolian Harp	*W. Allingham*	50
The Sea Limits	*Dante G. Rossetti*	51
To Daffodils	*R. Herrick*	52
Three Sonnets	*R. Buchanan*	53
In the Shadows	*David Gray*	54
The Moon	*W. B. Scott*	55
A Symbol	*W. B. Scott*	56
Declension and Revival	*Dora Greenwell*	56
February 1st, 1842	*Hartley Coleridge*	57
A Summer Wish	*Christina Rossetti*	58
October	*Arthur Munby*	59
The Rainbow	*Henry Vaughan*	60
A Drop of Dew	*Andrew Marvell*	61
Virtue	*George Herbert*	62
The Evening Cloud	*John Wilson*	63
Parting Gleams	*Aubrey de Vere*	64

BOOK SECOND.—LIFE.

DUTY.

Ode to Duty	*Wordsworth*	67
The Right must Win	*F. W. Faber*	69

PAGE

The Manly Life . . . . . . *Henry More* 71
On his Twenty-third Year . . . . *Milton* 72
On his Blindness . . . . . . *Milton* 72
London, 1802 . . . . . . *Wordsworth* 73
Not made in Vain . . . . *Hartley Coleridge* 74.
Self-dependence . . . . . *Matthew Arnold* 74
Morality . . . . . . *Matthew Arnold* 76
All-Saints . . . . . . *J. R. Lowell* 77
Good Life, Long Life . . . . . *Ben Jonson* 78
I will arise . . . . . *Songs of Two Worlds* 79
Flowers without Fruit . . . . *J. H. Newman* 80
Work and Contemplation . . . *E. B. Browning* 81
A Christmas Carol . . . . . *C. Kingsley* 82
Every-day . . . . . . *W. Allingham* 83
Pusillanimity . . . . . . *J. H. Newman* 85
Sensitiveness . . . . . *J. H. Newman* 85

DISCIPLINE.

Semita Justorum . . . . . *J. H. Newman* 87
Man . . . . *Henry Vaughan* 88
The Pulley . . . . . . *George Herbert* 89
The Collar . . . . . . *George Herbert* 90
Joy in Sorrow . . . . *C. H. Townshend* 91
Five Sonnets . . . . . *G. MacDonald* 92
A Day's Release . . . . . *Coventry Patmore* 94
Against Tears . . . . . *Sarah Williams* 95
Weariness . . . . . . *F. A. Kemble* 96
Mourner that dost deserve . . . . *Anonymous* 97
A Dream of the Cross . . . . *G. MacDonald* 97
Isolation . . . . . . *Jean Ingelow* 99
Exaggeration . . . . . *E. B. Browning* 100
Finite and Infinite . . . . *E. B. Browning* 101
The Messenger . . . . . *W. Allingham* 101

PENITENCE.

Levavi Oculos . . . . . *W. Allingham* 103

LOVE.

PAGE

The Kingdom of God . . . . *R. C. Trench* 176
Loved Once . . . . . *E. B. Browning* 177
Faith, Hope, and Charity . . . *Aubrey de Vere* 180
Enosis . . . . . . *C. P. Cranch* 180
Love's Deep Life . . . . *J. R. Lowell* 182
Love in Tears . . . . *Coventry Patmore* 182
An Angel in the House . . . . *Leigh Hunt* 183
Love in thy Heart . . . *William C. Roscoe* 184
To my Mother . . . . *William C. Roscoe* 184
Love on Earth . . . . . *Jean Ingelow* 185
To a Friend . . . . . *Hartley Coleridge* 186
The Revelation . . . . *Coventry Patmore* 186
What were I, Love . . . . *J. R. Lowell* 187
Eternal Love . . . . *Sir Philip Sidney* 188

PEACE.

The Peace of God . . . . *A. A. Procter* 189
The Sleep . . . . . *E. B. Browning* 190
The Starry Skies . . . . *F. W. Faber* 192
The Night . . . . . *Henry Vaughan* 196
Longing . . . . . . *G. MacDonald* 197
Like Morning . . . . *William C. Roscoe* 199
The Guardian Angel . . . . *R. Browning* 199
O Happy Days . . . . . *R. C. Trench* 201
Comfort . . . . . *E. B. Browning* 202
Per Pacem ad Lucem . . . . *A. A. Procter* 203

CHANGES, REGRETS, LONGINGS.

Mutability . . . . . . *Wordsworth* 204
Eutopia . . . . . . *F. T. Palgrave* 205
Youth and Age . . . . . *S. T. Coleridge* 205
Irreparableness . . . . *E. B. Browning* 207
The Buried Life . . . . *Matthew Arnold* 208
The Fire of Driftwood . . *H. W. Longfellow* 211
Qua Cursum Ventus . . . . *A. H. Clough* 213

PAGE

A Superscription . . . . . *Dante G. Rossetti* 215
A Song against Singing . . . *E. B. Browning* 215
The Happy Hearts of Earth . . *R. Buchanan* 217
Father, forgive thy Child . . . *R. Buchanan* 218
Vestigia retrorsum . . . . *Arthur Munby* 218
The Prisoner . . . . . *E. B. Browning* 219
Broken Music . , . . *Dante G. Rossetti* 220
Aspiration . . . . . . *T. Burbidge* 220
A Cry for Rest . . . . . *F. A. Kemble* 222
Friends of my Youth . . . *Mrs. Archer Clive* 222
Home . . . . . . *W. E. Channing* 223

THE JOURNEY.

The Future . . . . . . *Matthew Arnold* 225
Where lies the Land . . . . *A. H. Clough* 228
Starlight . . . . . *Mrs. Archer Clive* 229
On the Sea Beach . . . . *H. D. Thoreau* 230
Life . . . . *A. L. Barbauld* 231
Up-hill . . . . . *Christina Rossetti* 231
At Noontide came a Voice . . . *Dora Greenwell* 232
Prospice . . . . . . *R. Browning* 233
The Golden Gate . . . . *A. A. Procter* 234
The Retreat . . . . . *Henry Vaughan* 236
Intimations of Immortality . . . *Wordsworth* 237

BOOK THIRD.—DEATH AND IMMORTALITY

Beyond the Veil . . . . . *Henry Vaughan* 247
Time's Book . . . . . *Henry Vaughan* 249
Consolations in Bereavement . . *J. H. Newman* 250
The Deserted House . . . . *Alfred Tennyson* 252
Fear of Death . . . . . *Sir Philip Sidney* 253
Give Pardon, blessed Soul . . . *Henry Constable* 254
Death, be not proud . . . . *John Donne* 254

		PAGE
Sweet Death	Christina Rossetti	255
Night and Death	J. Blanco White	256
Desideria	Wordsworth	257
The Lullaby	W. Allingham	257
Fire	J. Keble	258
Death of two little Children	C. Turner	260
On an Infant	S. T. Coleridge	261
Death of Babe Christabel	Gerald Massey	261
Evelyn Hope	R. Browning	264
Gone	J. G. Whittier	266
The Death-Bed	T. Hood	269
Released	Adeline D. T. Whitney	270
I cannot think	J. R. Lowell	271
Soul of my Friend	T. Burbidge	272
Burial of the Dead	J. Keble	272
Guiding Stars	Henry Vaughan	275
River that stealest	H. W. Longfellow	276
Consolation	E. B. Browning	277
After my Sister's Death	William C. Roscoe	277
To a Friend	William C. Roscoe	279
Why fear	William C. Roscoe	280
A Voice from afar	J. H. Newman	281
Dirge	R. W. Emerson	281
My Mother	W. B. Scott	284
May and Death	R. Browning	284
An Anniversary	T. Burbidge	285
Dear Friend, far off	Alfred Tennyson	287
How pure at heart	Alfred Tennyson	288
The Prospect	E. B. Browning	289
Suspiria	H. W. Longfellow	289
O living will	Alfred Tennyson	290

BOOK I

NATURE.

Gifts.

———◆———

THE INNER VISION.

MOST sweet it is with unuplifted eyes
　　To pace the ground, if path there be or none,
While a fair region round the traveller lies
Which he forbears again to look upon;
Pleased rather with some soft ideal scene,
The work of fancy, or some happy tone
Of meditation, slipping in between
The beauty coming and the beauty gone.
If Thought and Love desert us, from that day
Let us break off all commerce with the Muse:
With Thought and Love companions of our way,
Whate'er the senses take or may refuse,
The Mind's internal heaven shall shed her dews
Of inspiration on the humblest lay.

WILLIAM WORDSWORTH.

THE GLORY OF NATURE.

I F only once the chariot of the morn
　　Had scattered from its wheels the twilight dun,
　　But once the unimaginable sun
Flashed godlike through perennial clouds forlorn,
And shown us beauty for a moment born;

If only once blind eyes had seen the Spring,
　　Waking amid the triumphs of mid-noon;
　　But once had seen the lovely Summer boon
Pass by in state like a full-robèd king,
The waters dance, the woodlands laugh and sing ⁝

If only once deaf ears had heard the joy
　　Of the wild birds, or morning breezes blowing,
　　Or silver fountains from their caverns flowing,
Or the deep-voicèd rivers rolling by;
Then night eternal fallen from the sky;

If only once weird Time had rent asunder
　　The curtain of the clouds, and shown us night
　　Climbing into the awful Infinite—
Those stairs whose steps are worlds, above and under,
Glory on glory, wonder upon wonder !

The lightnings lit the earthquake on his way ;
　　The sovran thunder spoken to the world;
　　The realm-wide banners of the wind unfurled ;
Earth-prisoned fires broke loose into the day ;
Or the great seas awoke—then slept for aye !—

Ah! sure the heart of man, too strongly tried
  By Godlike Presences so vast and fair,
  Withering with dread, or sick with love's despair,
Had wept for ever and to Heaven cried,
Or, struck with lightnings of delight, had died.

But he, though heir of Immortality,
  With mortal dust too feeble for the sight,
  Draws through a veil God's overwhelming light;
Use arms the soul—anon there moveth by
A more majestic angel—and we die!

FREDERICK TENNYSON.

THE LATTICE AT SUNRISE.

AS on my bed at dawn I mused and prayed,
   I saw my lattice prankt upon the wall,
The flaunting leaves and flitting birds withal—
A sunny phantom interlaced with shade.
'Thanks be to heaven,' in happy mood I said,
'What sweeter aid my matins could befall
Than this fair glory from the East hath made?
What holy sleights hath God, the Lord of all,
To bid us feel and see! We are not free
To say we see not, for the glory comes
Nightly and daily, like the flowing sea;
His lustre pierceth through the midnight glooms;
And, at prime hour, behold! He follows me
With golden shadows to my secret rooms!'

CHARLES TURNER.

THE FOREST GLADE.

A S, one dark morn, I trod a forest glade,
   A sunbeam entered at the further end,
And ran to meet me through the yielding shade—
As one who in the distance sees a friend,
And, smiling, hurries to him ; but mine eyes,
Bewildered by the change from dark to bright,
Received the greeting with a quick surprise
At first, and then with tears of pure delight :
For sad my thoughts had been—the tempest's wrath
Had gloomed the night, and made the morrow grey ;
That heavenly guidance humble sorrow hath
Had turned my feet into that forest-way,
Just when His morning light came down the path,
Among the lonely woods at early day.

CHARLES TURNER.

MAY CAROLS.

I.

W HO feels not, when the Spring once more,
   Stepping o'er Winter's grave forlorn,
With wingèd feet retreads the shore
   Of widowed earth, his bosom burn ?

As ordered flower succeeds to flower,
   And May the ladder of her sweets
Ascends, advancing hour by hour
   From scale to scale, what heart but beats ?

Some Presence veiled, in fields and groves,
    That mingles rapture with remorse,
Some buried joy beside us moves,
    And thrills the soul with such discourse

As they, perchance, that wondering pair
    Who to Emmaus bent their way,
Hearing, heard not; like them our prayer
    We make—'The night is near us. . Stay !'

With Paschal chants the churches ring,
    Their echoes strike along the tombs;
The birds their Hallelujahs sing;
    Each flower with floral incense fumes.

Our long-lost Eden seems restored ;
    As on we move with tearful eyes
We feel through all the illumined sward
    Some upward-working Paradise.

II.

Three worlds there are :—the first of Sense—
    That sensuous earth which round us lies;
The next of Faith's Intelligence ;
    The third of Glory, in the skies.

The first is palpable, but base ;
    The second heavenly, but obscure;
The third is starlike in the face—
    But ah ! remote that world as pure!

Yet, glancing through our misty clime,
  Some sparkles from that loftier sphere
Make way to earth ;—then most what time
  The annual spring-flowers reappear.

Amid the coarser needs of earth
  All shapes of brightness, what are they
But wanderers exiled from their birth,
  Or pledges of a happier day?

Yea, what is beauty, judged aright,
  But some surpassing, transient gleam ;
Some smile from heaven, in waves of light,
  Rippling o'er life's distempered dream?

Or broken memories of that bliss
  Which rushed thro' first-born Nature's blood
When He who ever was and is
  Looked down and saw that all was good?

                          AUBREY DE VERE.

THE DAFFODILS.

I WANDERED lonely as a cloud
    That floats on high o'er vales and hills
When all at once I saw a crowd,
    A host, of golden daffodils,
Beside the lake, beneath the trees,
Fluttering and dancing in the breeze.

Continuous as the stars that shine
   And twinkle on the milky way,
They stretched in never-ending line
   Along the margin of a bay :
Ten thousand saw I at a glance,
Tossing their heads in sprightly dance.

The waves beside them danced ; but they
   Out-did the sparkling waves in glee :
A poet could not but be gay
   In such a jocund company !
I gazed—and gazed—but little thought
What wealth the show to me had brought:

For oft, when on my couch I lie
   In vacant or in pensive mood,
They flash upon that inward eye
   Which is the bliss of solitude ;
And then my heart with pleasure fills,
And dances with the daffodils.

                WILLIAM WORDSWORTH.

EVENTIDE.

COMES something down with eventide,
   Beside the sunset's golden bars,
Beside the floating scents, beside
   The twinkling shadows of the stars.

Upon the river's rippling face,
Flash after flash, the white
Broke up in many a shallow place;
The rest was soft and bright.

By chance my eye fell on the stream:
—How many a marvellous power
Sleeps in us—sleeps, and doth not dream!
This knew I in that hour.

For then my heart, so full of strife,
No more was in me stirred;
My life was in the river's life,
And I nor saw nor heard.

I and the river, we were one:
The shade beneath the bank,
I felt it cool; the setting sun
Into my spirit sank.

A rushing thing in power serene
I was; the mystery
I felt of having ever been,
And being still to be.

Was it a moment or an hour?
I know not; but I mourned
When, from that realm of awful power,
I to these fields returned.

THOMAS BURBIDGE.

MAN.

M Y God, I heard this day
　　That none doth build a stately
　　　habitation
But he that means to dwell therein.
What house more stately hath there been,
Or can be, than is Man? to whose creation
　　All things are in decay.

　　For Man is every thing,
And more.　He is a tree, yet bears no fruit ;
　　A beast, yet is, or should be, more :
　　Reason and speech we only bring.
Parrots may thank us if they are not mute,
　　They go upon the score.

　　Man is all symmetry,
Full of proportions, one limb to another,
　　And all to all the world besides :
　　Each part may call the farthest, brother ;
For head with foot hath private amity,
　　And both with moons and tides.

　　Nothing hath got so far
But man hath caught and kept it as his prey.
　　His eyes dismount the highest star ;
　　He is in little all the sphere.
Herbs gladly cure our flesh, because that they
　　Find their acquaintance there.

For us the winds do blow,
The earth doth rest, heaven move, and fountains flow ;
Nothing we see but means our good,
As our delight, or as our treasure.
The whole is either our cupboard of food
Or cabinet of pleasure.

The stars have us to bed ;
Night draws the curtain which the sun withdraws :
Music and light attend our head.
All things unto our flesh are kind
In their descent and being ; to our mind
In their ascent and cause.

Each thing is full of duty :
Waters united are our navigation ;
Distinguished, our habitation ;
Below, our drink ; above, our meat :
Both are our cleanliness.   Hath one such beauty ?
Then how are all things neat !

More servants wait on man
Than he'll take notice of : in every path
He treads down that which doth befriend him
When sickness makes him pale and wan.
Oh mighty love ! Man is one world, and hath
Another to attend him.

Since then, my God, Thou hast
So brave a palace built, oh dwell in it,
That it may dwell with Thee at last !

Till then, afford us so much wit
That, as the world serves us, we may serve Thee,
And both thy servants be.

GEORGE HERBERT.

IN EARLY SPRING.

I HEARD a thousand blended notes,
  While in a grove I sat reclined,
In that sweet mood when pleasant thoughts
  Bring sad thoughts to the mind.

To her fair works did Nature link
  The human soul that through me ran;
And much it grieved my heart to think
  What man has made of man.

Through primrose tufts, in that green bower,
  The periwinkle trailed its wreaths;
And 'tis my faith that every flower
  Enjoys the air it breathes.

The birds around me hopped and played,
  Their thoughts I cannot measure—
But the least motion which they made
  It seemed a thrill of pleasure.

The budding twigs spread out their fan
  To catch the breezy air;
And I must think, do all I can,
  That there was pleasure there.

If this belief from heaven be sent,
If such be Nature's holy plan,
Have I not reason to lament
What man has made of man?

WILLIAM WORDSWORTH.

EACH AND ALL.

L ITTLE thinks, in the field, yon red-cloaked clown
   Of thee from the hill-top looking down;
The heifer that lows on the upland farm,
Far-heard, lows not thine ear to charm;
The sexton, tolling his bell at noon,
Deems not that great Napoleon
Stops his horse, and lists with delight,
Whilst his files sweep round yon alpine height;
Nor knowest thou what argument
Thy life to thy neighbour's creed has lent.
All are needed by each one;
Nothing is fair or good alone.

I thought the sparrow's note from heaven,
Singing at dawn on the alder bough;
I brought him home in his nest at even;—
He sings the song, but it pleases not now;
For I did not bring home the river and sky.
He sang to my ear; they sang to my eye.

The delicate shells lay on the shore;
The bubbles of the latest wave
Fresh pearls to their enamel gave;

And the bellowing of the savage sea
Greeted their safe escape to me.
I wiped away the weeds and foam,
I fetched my sea-born treasures home;
But the poor, unsightly, noisome things
Had left their beauty on the shore
With the sun, and the sand, and the wild uproar.

The lover watched his graceful maid,
As 'mid the virgin train she strayed,
Nor knew her beauty's best attire
Was woven still by the snow-white choir.
At last she came to his hermitage,
Like the bird from the woodlands to the cage;—
The gay enchantment was undone,—
A gentle wife, but fairy none.

Then I said 'I covet Truth;
Beauty is unripe childhood's cheat,—
I leave it behind with the games of youth.'
As I spoke, beneath my feet
The ground-pine curled its pretty wreath,
Running over the club-moss burrs;
I inhaled the violet's breath:
Around me stood the oaks and firs;
Pine-cones and acorns lay on the ground;
Over me soared the eternal sky,
Full of light and deity.
Again I saw, again I heard,
The rolling river, the morning bird:

Beauty through my senses stole;
I yielded myself to the perfect whole.

RALPH WALDO EMERSON.

THE RAINBOW.

M Y heart leaps up when I behold
　　A rainbow in the sky:
So was it when my life began;
So is it now I am a man;
So be it when I shall grow old—
　　Or let me die!
The Child is father of the Man;
And I could wish my days to be
Bound each to each by natural piety.

WILLIAM WORDSWORTH.

AN EVENING VOLUNTARY.

Composed upon an evening of extraordinary splendour and beauty.

I.

H AD this effulgence disappeared
　　With flying haste, I might have sent,
Among the speechless clouds, a look
Of blank astonishment;
But 'tis endued with power to stay,
And sanctify one closing day,
That frail mortality may see—
What is?—ah no, but what *can* be!

Time was when field and watery cove
With modulated echoes rang,
While choirs of fervent angels sang
Their vespers in the grove ;
Or, crowning, star-like, each some sovereign height,
Warbled, for heaven above and earth below,
Strains suitable to both.—Such holy rite,
Methinks, if audibly repeated now
From hill or valley, could not move
Sublimer transport, purer love,
Than doth this silent spectacle—the gleam—
The shadow—and the peace supreme.

II.

No sound is uttered,—but a deep
And solemn harmony pervades
The hollow vale from steep to steep,
And penetrates the glades.
Far-distant images draw nigh,
Called forth by wondrous potenc
Of beamy radiance, that imbues
Whate'er it strikes with gem-like hues !
In vision exquisitely clear,
Herds range along the mountain side ;
And glistening antlers are descried,
And gilded flocks appear.
Thine is the tranquil hour, purpureal eve !
But long as god-like wish, or hope divine,
Informs my spirit, ne'er can I believe
That this magnificence is wholly thine !

C

From worlds not quickened by the sun
A portion of the gift is won;
An intermingling of Heaven's pomp is spread
On ground which British shepherds tread!

III.

And, if there be whom broken ties
Afflict, or injuries assail,
Yon hazy ridges to their eyes
Present a glorious scale,
Climbing suffused with sunny air,
To stop—no record hath told where!
And tempting fancy to ascend,
And with immortal Spirits blend!
—Wings at my shoulders seem to play;
But, rooted here, I stand and gaze
On those bright steps that heavenward raise
Their practicable way.
Come forth, ye drooping old men, look abroad,
And see to what fair countries ye are bound!
And if some traveller, weary of his road,
Hath slept since noon-tide on the grassy ground,
Ye Genii! to his covert speed,
And wake him with such gentle heed
As may attune his soul to meet the dower
Bestowed on this transcendent hour!

IV.

Such hues from their celestial urn
Were wont to stream before mine eye,
Where'er it wandered in the morn
Of blissful infancy.

This glimpse of glory why renewed ?
Nay, rather speak with gratitude ;
For, if a vestige of those gleams
Survived, 'twas only in my dreams.
Dread Power ! whom peace and calmness serve
No less than Nature's threatening voice,
If aught unworthy be my choice,
From THEE if I would swerve ;
Oh ! let thy grace remind me of the light
Full early lost, and fruitlessly deplored,
Which, at this moment, on my waking sight
Appears to shine, by miracle restored ;
My soul, though yet confined to earth,
Rejoices in a second birth !
—'Tis past ! the visionary splendour fades,
And Night approaches with her shades.

WILLIAM WORDSWORTH.

THE LAST DAY OF AUTUMN.

THE year lies dying in this evening light ;
    The poet, musing in autumnal woods,
      Hears melancholy sighs
      Among the withered leaves.

Not so—but like a spirit glorified
The angel of the year departs, lays down
      His robes, once green in spring,
      Or bright with summer's blue,

And, having done his mission on the earth,
Filling ten thousand vales with golden corn,
    Orchards with rosy fruit,
    And scattering flowers around,—

He lingers for a moment in the west,
With the declining sun sheds over all
    A pleasant, farewell smile,
    And so returns to God.

FROM THE GERMAN.

BY THE SEA.

IT is a beautous evening, calm and free ;
    The holy time is quiet as a nun
Breathless with adoration ; the broad sun
Is sinking down in its tranquillity ;
The gentleness of heaven is on the sea :
Listen ! the mighty being is awake,
And doth with his eternal motion make
A sound like thunder—everlastingly.
Dear child ! dear girl ! that walkest with me here,
If thou appear untouched by solemn thought,
Thy nature is not therefore less divine :
Thou liest in Abraham's bosom all the year,
And worship'st at the Temple's inner shrine,
God being with thee when we know it not.

WILLIAM WORDSWORTH.

LINES

Composed a few miles above Tintern Abbey, on re-visiting the
banks of the Wye during a tour, July 13th, 1798.

FIVE years have past; five summers, with the
    length
Of five long winters! and again I hear
These waters, rolling from their mountain-springs
With a soft inland murmur.   Once again
Do I behold these steep and lofty cliffs,
That on a wild secluded scene impress
Thoughts of more deep seclusion, and connect
The landscape with the quiet of the sky.
The day is come when I again repose
Here, under this dark sycamore, and view
These plots of cottage ground, these orchard-tufts,
Which, at this season, with their unripe fruits,
Are clad in one green hue, and lose themselves
'Mid groves and copses.   Once again I see
These hedge-rows, hardly hedge-rows, little lines
Of sportive wood run wild : these pastoral farms,
Green to the very door; and wreaths of smoke
Sent up, in silence, from among the trees !
With some uncertain notice, as might seem,
Of vagrant dwellers in the houseless woods,
Or of some hermit's cave, where, by his fire,
The hermit sits alone.

                  These beauteous forms,
Through a long absence, have not been to me
As is a landscape to a blind man's eye :

But oft, in lonely rooms, and 'mid the din
Of towns and cities, I have owed to them
In hours of weariness, sensations sweet,
Felt in the blood, and felt along the heart ;
And passing even into my purer mind,
With tranquil restoration :—feelings too
Of unremembered pleasure : such, perhaps,
As have no slight or trivial influence
On that best portion of a good man's life,
His little, nameless, unremembered acts
Of kindness and of love.   Nor less, I trust,
To them I may have owed another gift,
Of aspect more sublime ; that blessed mood,
In which the burden of the mystery,
In which the heavy and the weary weight
Of all this unintelligible world,
Is lightened :—that serene and blessed mood,
In which the affections gently lead us on,
Until, the breath of this corporeal frame
And even the motion of our human blood
Almost suspended, we are laid asleep
In body, and become a living soul :
While, with an eye made quiet by the power
Of harmony, and the deep power of joy,
We see into the life of things.
                                        If this
Be but a vain belief, yet, oh ! how oft—
In darkness and amid the many shapes
Of joyless daylight ; when the fretful stir
Unprofitable, and the fever of the world,

Have hung upon the beatings of my heart—
How oft, in spirit, have I turned to thee,
O sylvan Wye! thou wanderer thro' the woods,
How often has my spirit turned to thee !
    And now, with gleams of half-extinguished thought,
With many recognitions dim and faint,
And somewhat of a sad perplexity,
The picture of the mind revives again :
While here I stand, not only with the sense
Of present pleasure, but with pleasing thoughts
That in this moment there is life and food
For future years.   And so I dare to hope,
Though changed, no doubt, from what I was when first
I came among these hills ; when, like a roe,
I bounded o'er the mountains, by the sides
Of the deep rivers, and the lonely streams,
Wherever nature led : more like a man
Flying from something that he dreads, than one
Who sought the thing he loved.   For nature then
(The coarser pleasures of my boyish days,
And their glad animal movements all gone by)
To me was all in all.   I cannot paint
What then I was.   The sounding cataract
Haunted me like a passion: the tall rock,
The mountain, and the deep and gloomy wood,
Their colours and their forms, were then to me
An appetite ; a feeling and a love,
That had no need of a remoter charm,
By thought supplied, nor any interest
Unborrowed from the eye.—That time is past,

And all its aching joys are now no more,
And all its dizzy raptures. Not for this
Faint I, nor mourn, nor murmur ; other gifts
Have followed ; for such loss, I would believe,
Abundant recompense. For I have learned
To look on nature, not as in the hour
Of thoughtless youth ; but hearing oftentimes
The still, sad music of humanity,
Nor harsh, nor grating, though of ample power
To chasten and subdue. And I have felt
A presence that disturbs me with the joy
Of elevated thoughts ; a sense sublime
Of something far more deeply interfused,
Whose dwelling is the light of setting suns,
And the round ocean and the living air,
And the blue sky, and in the mind of man :
A motion and a spirit, that impels
All thinking things, all objects of all thought,
And rolls through all things. Therefore am I still
A lover of the meadows and the woods,
And mountains ; and of all that we behold
From this green earth ; of all the mighty world
Of eye, and ear,—both what they half-create,
And what perceive ; well pleased to recognize
In nature and the language of the sense
The anchor of my purest thoughts, the nurse,
The guide, the guardian of my heart, and soul
Of all my moral being.
                              Nor, perchance,
If I were not thus taught, should I the more

Suffer my genial spirits to decay :
For thou art with me here upon the banks
Of this fair river ; thou, my dearest friend,
My dear, dear friend ; and in thy voice I catch
The language of my former heart and read
My former pleasures in the shooting lights
Of thy wild eyes. Oh ! yet a little while
May I behold in thee what I was once,
My dear, dear sister ! and this prayer I make,
Knowing that Nature never did betray
The heart that loved her ; 'tis her privilege,
Through all the years of this our life, to lead
From joy to joy ; for she can so inform
The mind that is within us, so impress
With quietness and beauty, and so feed
With lofty thoughts, that neither evil tongues,
Rash judgments, nor the sneers of selfish men,
Nor greetings where no kindness is, nor all
The dreary intercourse of daily life,
Shall e'er prevail against us or disturb
Our cheerful faith, that all which we behold
Is full of blessings. Therefore let the moon
Shine on thee in thy solitary walk ;
And let the misty mountain-winds be free
To blow against thee : and, in after years,
When these wild ecstasies shall be matured
Into a sober pleasure ; when thy mind
Shall be a mansion for all lovely forms,
Thy memory be as a dwelling-place
For all sweet sounds and harmonies ; oh ! then,

If solitude, or fear, or pain, or grief,
Should be thy portion, with what healing thoughts
Of tender joy wilt thou remember me,
And these my exhortations ! Nor, perchance,
If I should be where I no more can hear
Thy voice, nor catch from thy wild eyes these gleams
Of past existence—wilt thou then forget
That on the banks of this delightful stream
We stood together ; and that I, so long
A worshipper of Nature, hither came,
Unwearied in that service : rather say
With warmer love—oh ! with far deeper zeal
Of holier love. Nor wilt thou then forget,
That after many wanderings, many years
Of absence, these steep woods and lofty cliffs,
And this green pastoral landscape, were to me
More dear, both for themselves and for thy sake !

WILLIAM WORDSWORTH.

Lessons.

THE BOOK OF THE WORLD.

OF this fair volume which we World do name
    If we the sheets and leaves could turn with care,
Of Him who it corrects, and did it frame,
We clear might read the art and wisdom rare;
Find out his power which wildest powers doth tame,
His providence extending everywhere,
His justice which proud rebels doth not spare—
In every page, no period of the same.
But silly we, like foolish children, rest
Well pleased with colour'd vellum, leaves of gold,
Fair dangling ribbands, leaving what is best,
On the great Writer's sense ne'er taking hold;
Or if, by chance, we stay our minds on aught,
It is some picture on the margin wrought.

WILLIAM DRUMMOND.

LOVE OF NATURE.

GLAD sight wherever new with old
    Is joined through some dear home-born tie;
The life of all that we behold
    Depends upon that mystery.
Vain is the glory of the sky,
    The beauty vain of field and grove,
Unless, while with admiring eye
    We gaze, we also learn to love.
                WILLIAM WORDSWORTH.

INSIGHT.

I GRIEVE not that ripe knowledge takes away
    The charm that Nature to my childhood wore,
For, with that insight, cometh, day by day,
A greater bliss than wonder was before;
The real doth not clip the poet's wings,—
To win the secret of a weed's plain heart
Reveals some clue to spiritual things,
And stumbling guess becomes firm-footed art.
Flowers are not flowers unto the poet's eyes;
Their beauty thrills him by an inward sense:
He knows that outward seemings are but lies,
Or, at the most, but earthly shadows, whence
The soul that looks within for truth may guess
The presence of some wondrous heavenliness.
                JAMES RUSSELL LOWELL.

LESSONS FROM THE GORSE.

'To win the secret of a weed's plain heart.'—LOWELL.

M OUNTAIN gorses, ever golden,
Cankered not the whole year long !
Do ye teach us to be strong,
Howsoever pricked and holden
Like your thorny blooms, and so
Trodden on by rain and snow,
Up the hill-side of this life, as bleak as where ye grow ?

Mountain blossoms, shining blossoms,
Do ye teach us to be glad
When no summer can be had,
Blooming in our inward bosoms ?
Ye, whom God preserveth still,
Set as lights upon a hill,
Tokens to the wintry earth that Beauty liveth still !

Mountain gorses, do ye teach us
From that academic chair
Canopied with azure air,
That the wisest word man reaches
Is the humblest he can speak ?
Ye, who live on mountain peak,
Yet live low along the ground, beside the grasses meek !

Mountain gorses, since Linnæus
Knelt beside you on the sod,
For your beauty thanking God,—

For your teaching, ye should see us
Bowing in prostration new !
Whence arisen,—if one or two
Drops be on our cheeks—O world, they are not tears
　　but dew.

　　　　　　　ELIZABETH BARRETT BROWNING.

MY DOVES.

'O Weisheit ! du red'st wie eine Taube !'—GOETHE.

M Y little doves have left a nest
　　　Upon an Indian tree,
Whose leaves fantastic take their rest,
　　Or motion, from the sea ;
For, ever there the sea-winds go
With sun-lit paces to and fro.

The tropic flowers looked up to it,
　　The tropic stars looked down,
And there my little doves did sit,
　　With feathers softly brown,
And glittering eyes that showed their right
To general Nature's deep delight.

And God them taught, at every close
　　Of murmuring waves beyond
And green leaves round, to interpose
　　Their choral voices fond,
Interpreting that love must be
The meaning of the earth and sea.

Fit ministers!   Of living loves
　　Theirs hath the calmest fashion,
Their living voice the likest moves
　　To lifeless intonation,
The lovely monotone of springs
And winds and such insensate things.

My little doves were ta'en away
　　From that glad nest of theirs,
Across an ocean rolling grey,
　　And tempest-clouded airs ;
My little doves, who lately knew
The sky and wave by warmth and blue.

And now, within the city prison,
　　In mist and chillness pent,
With sudden upward look they listen
　　For sounds of past content,
For lapse of water, swell of breeze,
Or nut-fruit falling from the trees.

The stir without the glow of passion,
　　The triumph of the mart,
The gold and silver as they clash on
　　Man's cold metallic heart,
The roar of wheels, the cry for bread,
These only sounds are heard instead.

Yet still, as on my human hand
　　Their fearless heads they lean,
And almost seem to understand ·
　　What human musings mean,

(Their eyes with such a plaintive shine
Are fastened upwardly to mine !)

Soft falls their chant as on the nest
    Beneath the sunny zone ;
For love that stirred it in their breast
    Has not aweary grown,
And 'neath the city's shade can keep
The well of music clear and deep.

And love, that keeps the music, fills
    With pastoral memories ;
All echoings from out the hills,
    All droppings from the skies,
All flowings from the wave and wind,
Remembered in their chant I find.

So teach ye me the wisest part,
    My little doves ! to move
Along the city ways with heart
    Assured by holy love,
And vocal with such songs as own
A fountain to the world unknown.

'Twas hard to sing by Babel's stream—
    More hard, in Babel's street :
But if the soulless creatures deem
    Their music not unmeet
For sunless walls—let *us* begin,
Who wear immortal wings within !

To me fair memories belong
　Of scenes that used to bless,
For no regret, but present song
　And lasting thankfulness,
And very soon to break away,
Like types, in purer things than they.

I will have hopes that cannot fade
　For flowers the valley yields ;
I will have humble thoughts instead
　Of silent, dewy fields :
My spirit and my God shall be
My sea-ward hill, my boundless sea.

ELIZABETH BARRETT BROWNING.

TO A WATERFOWL.

WHITHER, 'midst falling dew,
　　While glow the heavens with the last steps
　　　of day,
Far through their rosy depths, dost thou pursue
　　Thy solitary way?

　　Vainly the fowler's eye
Might mark thy distant flight to do thee wrong,
As, darkly limned upon the crimson sky,
　　Thy figure floats along.

　　Seek'st thou the plashy brink
Of weedy lake, or marge of river wide,

D

Or where the rocking billows rise and sink
  On the chafed ocean side?

    There is a Power whose care
Teaches thy way along that pathless coast—
The desert and illimitable air,—
    Lone wandering, but not lost.

    All day thy wings have fanned,
At that far height, the cold, thin atmosphere;
Yet stoop not, weary, to the welcome land,
    Though the dark night is near.

    And soon that toil shall end;
Soon shalt thou find a summer home, and rest,
And scream among thy fellows; reeds shall bend
    Soon o'er thy sheltered rest.

    Thou'rt gone, the abyss of heaven
Hath swallowed up thy form; yet on my heart
Deeply hath sunk the lesson thou hast given,
    And shall not soon depart.

    He who, from zone to zone,
Guides through the boundless sky thy certain flight,
In the long way that I must tread alone
    Will lead my steps aright.
                    WILLIAM CULLEN BRYANT.

THE REDBREAST IN SEPTEMBER.

THE morning mist is cleared away,
　　Yet still the face of heaven is grey,
Nor yet the autumnal breeze has stirred the grove ;
　　Faded, yet full, a paler green
　　Skirts soberly the tranquil scene ;
The redbreast warbles round this leafy cove.

　　Sweet messenger of calm decay,
　　Saluting sorrow as you may,
As one still bent to find or make the best,
　　In thee, and in this quiet mead,
　　The lesson of sweet peace I read,
Rather, in all, to be resigned than blest.

　　'Tis a low chant, according well
　　With the soft solitary knell,
As homeward from some grave beloved we turn,
　　Or by some holy death-bed dear,
　　Most welcome to the chastened ear
Of her whom Heaven is teaching how to mourn.

　　O cheerful tender strain ! the heart
　　That duly bears with you its part,
Singing, so thankful, to the dreary blast,
　　Though gone and spent its joyous prime,
　　And on the world's autumnal time,
'Mid withered hues and sere, its lot be cast :

That is the heart for thoughtful seer,
· Watching, in trance nor dark nor clear,
The appalling future as it nearer draws ;
      His spirit calmed the storm to meet,
      Feeling the rock beneath his feet,
And tracing through the cloud the eternal Cause.

      That is the heart for watchman true
      Waiting to see what God will do,
As o'er the church the gathering twilight falls :
      No more he strains his wistful eye,
      If chance the golden hours be nigh,
By youthful Hope seen beaming round her walls.

      Forced from his shadowy paradise,
      His thoughts to heaven the steadier rise :
There seek his answer when the world reproves :
      Contented in his darkling round,
      If only he be faithful found
When from the east the eternal morning moves.

                                JOHN KEBLE.

THE NIGHTINGALE.

L ESSONS sweet of Spring returning,
      Welcome to the thoughtful heart !
May I call ye sense, or learning,
      Instinct pure, or heaven-taught art ?

Be your title what it may,
Sweet the lengthening April day,
While with you the soul is free,
Ranging wild o'er hill and lea.

Soft as Memnon's harp at morning,
    To the inward ear devout,
Touched by light, with heavenly warning
    Your transporting chords ring out.
Every leaf in every nook,
Every wave in every brook,
Chanting with a solemn voice,
Minds us of our better choice.

Needs no show of mountain hoary,
    Winding shore, or deepening glen,
Where the landscape in its glory
    Teaches truth to wandering men :
Give true hearts but earth and sky,
And some flowers to bloom and die,—
Homely scenes and simple views,
Lowly thoughts may best infuse.

See the soft green willow springing
    Where the waters gently pass,
Every way her free arms flinging
    O'er the moist and reedy grass.
Long ere winter blasts are fled,
See her tipped with vernal red,

And her kindly flower displayed
Ere her leaf can cast a shade.

Though the rudest hand assail her,
　Patiently she droops awhile ;
But, when showers and breezes hail her,
　Wears again her willing smile.
Thus I learn contentment's power
From the slighted willow bower,
Ready to give thanks and live
On the least that Heaven may give.

If, the quiet brooklet leaving,
　Up the stony vale I wind,
Haply, half in fancy grieving
　For the shades I leave behind,
By the dusty wayside drear,
Nightingales with joyous cheer
Sing, my sadness to reprove,
Gladlier than in cultured grove.

Where the thickest boughs are twining
　Of the greenest, darkest tree,
There they plunge, the light declining—
　All may hear, but none may see.
Fearless of the passing hoof,
Hardly will they fleet aloof;
So they live in modest ways,
Trust entire, and ceaseless praise.

JOHN KEBLE.

COMPOSED DURING A STORM.

ONE who was suffering tumult in his soul,
   Yet failed to seek the sure relief of prayer,
Went forth—his course surrendering to the care
Of the fierce wind, while mid-day lightnings prowl
Insidiously, untimely thunders growl ;
While trees, dim-seen, in frenzied numbers, tear
The lingering remnant of their yellow hair,
And shivering wolves, surprised with darkness, howl
As if the sun were not.   He raised his eye,
Soul-smitten ; for, that instant, did appear
Large space, 'mid dreadful clouds, of purest sky,
An azure disc—shield of tranquillity ;
Invisible, unlooked-for, minister
Of providential goodness ever nigh !

WILLIAM WORDSWORTH.

THE CONSTELLATION OF THE PLOUGH.

TYPE of celestial labour, toil divine,
   That nightly downward from the glistening skies
Showerest thy light on these expectant eyes !
Around thee, in their stations, ever shine
Full many a radiant shape and emblemed sign ;
Swords, sceptres, crowns, bright tresses, galaxies
Of all that soaring fancy can devise—
Yet none, methinks, so truly great as thine !

On, ever on ! while He who guides thee flings
His golden grain along the azure way
Do thou thy sleepless work and, toiling, say, .
' O men, so sedulous in trivial things,
Why faint amid your loftier labours ?   Why
Forget the starry seed, and harvests of the sky?'

AUBREY DE VERE.

QUIET WORK.

ONE lesson, Nature, let me learn of thee,
    One lesson which in every wind is blown,
One lesson of two duties kept at one,
Though the loud world proclaim their enmity—
Of toil unsevered from tranquillity ;
Of labour, that in lasting fruit outgrows
Far noisier schemes, accomplished in repose—
Too great for haste, too high for rivalry.
Yes, while on earth a thousand discords ring,
Man's senseless uproar mingling with his toil,
Still do thy quiet ministers move on,
Their glorious tasks in silence perfecting !
Still working, blaming still our vain turmoil ;
Labourers that shall not fail, when man is gone.

MATTHEW ARNOLD.

Symbols.

———•———

TO A SKYLARK.

E THEREAL minstrel ! pilgrim of the sky !
Dost thou despise the earth where cares abound ?
Or, while the wings aspire, are heart and eye
Both with thy nest upon the dewy ground ?
Thy nest which thou canst drop into at will,
Those quivering wings composed, that music still.

To the last point of vision, and beyond,
Mount, daring warbler !—that love-prompted strain,
('Twixt thee and thine a never-failing bond)
Thrills not the less the bosom of the plain :
Yet might'st thou seem, proud privilege ! to sing
All independent of the leafy Spring.

Leave to the nightingale her shady wood ;
A privacy of glorious light is thine,
Whence thou dost pour upon the world a flood
Of harmony, with instinct more divine ;
Type of the wise who soar but never roam,
True to the kindred points of Heaven and Home.

WILLIAM WORDSWORTH.

THE SOUND OF THE SEA.

THE sea awoke at midnight from its sleep,
   And round the pebbly beaches far and wide
I heard the first wave of the rising tide
Rush onward with uninterrupted sweep—
A voice out of the silence of the deep,
   A sound mysteriously multiplied
   As of a cataract from the mountain's side,
Or roar of winds upon a wooded steep.
So comes to us at times, from the unknown
   And inaccessible solitudes of being,
   The rushing of the sea-tides of the soul;
And inspirations, that we deem our own,
   Are some divine foreshadowing and foreseeing
   Of things beyond our reason and control.
         HENRY WADSWORTH LONGFELLOW.

THE TROSACHS.

THERE'S not a nook within this solemn Pass
   But were an apt confessional for one
Taught by his summer spent, his autumn gone,
That life is but a tale of morning grass
Withered at eve.   From scenes of art which chase
That thought away, turn, and with watchful eyes
Feed it 'mid Nature's old felicities,
Rocks, rivers, and clear lakes more smooth than glass

Untouched, unbreathed upon.   Thrice happy quest
If, from a golden perch of aspen spray
(October's workmanship to rival May)
The pensive warbler of the ruddy breast
That moral sweeten by a heaven-taught lay,
Lulling the year with all its cares to rest.

WILLIAM WORDSWORTH.

A MAY CAROL.

H ERE, in this paradise of light,
  Superfluous were both tree and grass
Enough to watch the sunbeams smite
  Yon white flower sole in the morass.

From his cold nest the skylark springs ;
  Sings, pauses, sings ; shoots up anew ;
Attains his topmost height, and sings
  Quiescent in his vault of blue.

With eyes half-closed I watch the lake,
  Flashed from whose plane the sun-sparks fly,
Like souls new-born that shoot and break
  From thy deep sea, Eternity !

Ripplings of sunlight from the wave
  Ascend the white rock, high and higher ;
Soft gurglings fill the satiate cave ;
  Soft airs amid the reeds expire.

All round the lone and luminous mere
   The dark world stretches far and free :
That skylark's song alone I hear ;
   That flashing wave alone I see.

O myriad Earth ! where'er a word
   Of thine makes way into the soul,
An echo million-fold is stirred ;
   Of thee the part is as the whole.

AUBREY DE VERE.

THE SKYLARK.

H OW the blithe Lark runs up the golden stair
   That leads through cloudy gates from heaven to
      earth,
And, all alone in the empyreal air,
   Fills it with jubilant sweet songs of mirth ;
      How far he seems, how far,
         With the light upon his wings !
      Is it a bird, or star,
         That shines and sings ?

What matter if the days be dark and frore,
   That sunbeam tells of other days to be,
And, singing in the light that floods him o'er,
   In joy he overtakes futurity ;
      Under cloud-arches vast
         He peeps, and sees behind
      Great Summer coming fast
         Adown the wind !

And now he dives into a rainbow's rivers,
  In streams of gold and purple he is drowned;
Shrilly the arrows of his song he shivers,
  As though the stormy drops were turned to sound;
      And now he issues through,
        He scales a cloudy tower,
      Faintly, like falling dew,
        His fast notes shower.

Let every wind be hushed, that I may hear
  The wondrous things he tells the world below;
Things that we dream of he is watching near,
  Hopes that we never dreamed he would bestow.
      Alas! the storm hath rolled
        Back the gold gates again,
      Or surely he had told
        All heaven to men!

So the victorious Poet sings alone,
  And fills with light his solitary home,
And through that glory sees new worlds foreshown,
  And hears high songs and triumphs yet to come;
      He waves the air of time
        With thrills of golden chords,
      And makes the world to climb
        On linkèd words.

What if his hair be grey, his eyes be dim,
  If wealth forsake him, and if friends be cold;
Wonder unbars her thousand gates to him,
  Truth never fails, nor beauty waxeth old;

More than he tells, his eyes
Behold, his spirit hears,
Of grief, and joy, and sighs
'Twixt joy and tears.

Blest is the man who with the sound of song
Can charm away the heartache, and forget
The frost of penury, and the stings of wrong,
And drown the fatal whisper of regret!
Darker are the abodes
Of kings, though his be poor,
While fancies, like the gods,
Pass through his door.

Singing thou scalest heaven upon thy wings,
Thou liftest a glad heart into the skies;
He maketh his own sunrise while he sings,
And turns the dusty earth to Paradise;
I see thee sail along
Far up the sunny streams;
Unseen, I hear his song,
I see his dreams.

Frederick Tennyson.

FLOWER AND FRUIT.

A LITTLE child lay on its mother's knee
In shade of summer boughs; and that fond
mother
Waved in one hand the flowers of a wild tree,
And a fair branch of fruitage in the other.

Longing he lay, and glancing his blue eyes
From one to other—for his will was loth
To fix its choice—he sighed his first-born sighs,
   Stretched out both arms, and would have clutched
   them both.

A grey old man peeped through the leaves, and blessed
   That lovely child—then sadly turned apart,
And, sitting down a little from the rest,
   Sighed, as he murmured thus to his own heart :—

Within the violet's cup no nectar flows,
   Though its rich breath fills the delighted air;
When the ripe fruit is glistening on the boughs,
   The lovely blossom is no longer there :

When the young sun is arming him at morn,
   His beauty makes sweet rainbows in the sky;
But, when his wheels are up the zenith borne,
   He hath no power for such soft magist'ry:

When the swift heart of the enchanted boy
   Speaks through his downy cheeks and starry eyes,
An hour of love is worth eternal joy,
   And beauty all the treasures of the wise;

But when the time-worn heart begins to bud
   With leaves of truth, like the autumnal green,
No pulse of rapture stirs the drowsy blood,
   Scarce stirring with the pulses that have been.

Ah me! in what immortal hour of time,
Under what star, in what enchanted weather,
In what new Eden, in what fairy clime,
Nature, shall thy perfections meet together?

When youthful hearts, rejoicing in their May,
Shall bide in cheerful faith the unborn hour,
And the wise spirit not regret the day
That brings the fruit, but takes away the flower?

When Hope and Love, so lavish of delight,
Shall laugh and sing, yet crown their early years
With those rare buds, more odorous than bright,
And that wise spirit, now the growth of tears?

Ah! vexed Life, there is no other wand
But Death's cold finger—take him for thy friend;
He leadeth Truth and Beauty hand in hand,
He brings thee Youth and Knowledge without end.

FREDERICK TENNYSON.

THE HONEYSUCKLE.

I PLUCKED a honeysuckle where
The hedge on high is quick with thorn,
And climbing for the prize, was torn,
And fouled my feet in quag water;
And by the thorns and by the wind
The blossom that I took was thinn'd,
And yet I found it sweet and fair.

Thence to a richer growth I came,
  Where, nursed in mellow intercourse,
  The honeysuckles sprang by scores,
Not harried like my single stem,
  All virgin lamps of scent and dew.
  So from my hand that first I threw,
Yet plucked not any more of them.

DANTE GABRIEL ROSSETTI.

SYMBOLS.

I WATCHED a rosebud very long,
  Brought on by dew and sun and shower,
  Waiting to see the perfect flower:
Then, when I thought it should be strong,
  It opened at the matin hour
And fell at evensong.

I watched a nest from day to day,
  A green nest full of pleasant shade,
  Wherein three speckled eggs were laid:
But when they should have hatched in May
  The two old birds had grown afraid
Or tired, and flew away.

Then, in my wrath, I broke the bough
  That I had tended so with care,
  Hoping its scent should fill the air:
I crushed the eggs, not heeding how
  Their ancient promise had been fair;
I would have vengeance now.

E

But the dead branch spoke from the sod,
  And the eggs answered me again :
  Because we failed dost thou complain ?
Is thy wrath just ? And what if God,
  Who waiteth for thy fruits in vain,
Should also take the rod ?
CHRISTINA ROSSETTI.

ÆOLIAN HARP.

WHAT is it that is gone, we fancied ours ?
  O what is lost that never may be told ?—
We stray all afternoon, and we may grieve
Until the perfect closing of the night.
Listen to us, thou grey autumnal eve,
Whose part is silence. At thy verge the clouds
Are broken into melancholy gold ;
The waifs of autumn and the feeble flowers
Glimmer along our woodlands in wet light ;
Because within thy deep thou hast the shrouds
Of joy and great adventure, waxing cold,
Which once, or so it seemed, were full of might.
Some power it was, that lives not with us now,
A thought we had, but could not, could not hold.
O sweetly, swiftly passed !—air sings and murmurs ;
Green leaves are gathering on the dewy bough :
O sadly, swiftly passed !—air sighs and mutters ;
Red leaves are dropping on the rainy mould.
Then comes the snow, unfeatured, vast, and white.
O what is gone from us, we fancied ours ?
WILLIAM ALLINGHAM.

THE SEA-LIMITS.

CONSIDER the sea's listless chime:
    Time's self it is, made audible,—
    The murmur of the earth's own shell.
Secret continuance sublime
    Is the sea's end : our sight may pass
    No furlong further.   Since time was,
This sound hath told the lapse of time.

No quiet, which is death's,—it hath
    The mournfulness of ancient life,
    Enduring always at dull strife.
As the world's heart of rest and wrath,
    Its painful pulse is in the sands.
    Last utterly, the whole sky stands,
Grey and not known, along its path.

Listen alone beside the sea,
    Listen alone among the woods ;
    These voices of twin solitudes
Shall have one sound alike to thee:
    Hark where the murmurs of thronged men
    Surge and sink back and surge again,—
Still the one voice of wave and tree.

Gather a shell from the strown beach
    And listen at its lips : they sigh
    The same desire and mystery,
The echo of the whole sea's speech.

E 2

And all mankind is thus at heart
Not any thing but what thou art :
And Earth, Sea, Man, are all in each.

DANTE GABRIEL ROSSETTI.

TO DAFFODILS.

FAIR Daffodils, we weep to see
   You haste away so soon ;
As yet the early-rising sun
Has not attained his noon :
      Stay, stay,
      Until the hasting day
         Has run
      But to the even-song ;
And, having prayed together, we
      Will go with you along !

We have short time to stay as you,
We have as short a spring ;
As quick a growth to meet decay
As you, or any thing :
      We die
      As your hours do ; and dry
         Away
      Like to the summer's rain,
Or as the pearls of morning dew,
      Ne'er to be found again.

ROBERT HERRICK.

THREE SONNETS.

THE MOTION OF THE MISTS.

H ERE by the sunless lake there is no air,
    Yet with how ceaseless motion, with how strange
  Flowing and fading, do the high mists range
The gloomy gorges of the mountains bare.
Some weary breathing never ceases there,—
    The ashen peaks can feel it hour by hour;
    The purple depths are darkened by its power;
A soundless breath, a trouble all things share
That feel it come and go.   See ! onward swim
    The ghostly mists, from silent land to land,
From gulf to gulf; now the whole air grows dim—
    Like living men, darkling a space, they stand.
But lo ! a Sunbeam, like the Cherubim,
    Scatters them onward with a flaming brand.

CORUISK.

I think this is the very stillest place
    On all God's earth, and yet no rest is here.
The vapours mirrored in the black loch's face
    Drift on like frantic shapes and disappear;
    A never-ceasing murmur in mine ear
Tells me of waters wild that flow and flow.
    There is no rest at all, afar or near,
Only a sense of things that moan and go.
And lo ! the still small life these limbs contain
    I feel flows on like those, restless and proud;

Before that breathing nought within my brain
    Pauses, but all drifts on like mist and cloud ;
Only the bald peaks and the stones remain,
    Frozen before Thee, desolate and bowed.

BUT WHITHER ?

And whither, O ye vapours ! do ye wend ?
    Stirred by that weary breathing, whither away ?
    And whither, O ye dreams ! that night and day
Drift o'er the troublous life, tremble, and blend
To broken lineaments of that far Friend,
    Whose strange breath's come and go ye feel so deep ?
    O Soul ! that hast no rest and seekest sleep,
Whither ? and will thy wanderings ever end ?
All things that be are full of a quick pain ;
    Onward we fleet, swift as the running rill,—
The vapours drift, the mists within the brain
    Float on obscuringly and haye no will.
Only the bare peaks and the stones remain,.
    These only,—and a God sublime and still.
                                    ROBERT BUCHANAN.

IN THE SHADOWS.

DIE down, O dismal day ! and let me live ;
        And come, blue deeps ! magnificently strown
With coloured clouds—large, light, and fugitive—
    By upper winds through pompous motions blown.

Now it is death in life—a vapour dense
  Creeps round my window till I cannot see
The far snow-shining mountains and the glens
  Shagging the mountain tops. O God! make free
This barren, shackled earth, so deadly cold.
  Breathe gently forth thy Spring, till Winter flies
In rude amazement, fearful and yet bold,
  While she performs her customed charities.
I weigh the loaded hours till life is bare—
O God! for one clear day, a snowdrop, and sweet air !

DAVID GRAY.

THE MOON.

HOW often and how vainly do we try
    To paint in words the dying of the day !
  Coming repose ennobling us, the play
Of fretted fire and gold afar and nigh.
This night seen from that western casement high,
  It was so terribly fair with cloudlet-sheaves,
  Amber and ruby burning through the leaves,
I said once more, It must not pass me by !

But when another hour the clock had told,
  I went to look again, and saw framed there,
  By fringing ivy like carved jet, the sky,
The void sky, silver-bright, so vast, so cold,
  The faint moon round as is Eternity,—
  I quite forgot the sunset's splendid glare.

WILLIAM BELL SCOTT.

A SYMBOL.

A T early morn I watched, scarce consciously,
Through the half-opened casement, the high
screen
Of our trees touched now by the bright'ning sheen
Of the ascending sun : the room was grey
And dim, with old things filled this many a day,
Closing me in, but those thick folds of trees
Shone in the fresh light, trembled in the breeze :
A shadow crossed them on its arrowy way
Cast by a flying bird I could not see ;
Then called a voice far off that seemed to say,
Come, we are here !   Such might or might not be
What the voice called, but then methought I knew
I was a soul new-born in death's dark clay,
Awakening to another life more true.

WILLIAM BELL SCOTT.

DECLENSION AND REVIVAL.

'From Me is thy fruit found.'

D IE to thy root, sweet flower !
If so God wills, die even to thy root ;
Live there awhile an uncomplaining, mute,
Blank life, with darkness wrapped about thy head,
And fear not for the silence round thee spread.
This is no grave, though thou among the dead
Are counted, but the Hiding-place of Power.
Die to thy root, sweet flower !

Spring from thy root, sweet flower !
When so God wills, spring even from thy root ;
Send through the earth's warm breast a quickened shoot;
Spread to the sunshine, spread unto the shower,
And lift into the sunny air thy dower
Of bloom and odour.   Life is on the plains,
And, in the woods, a sound of buds and rains
That sing together.   Lo ! the winter's cold
Is past, sweet scents revive, thick buds unfold ;
Be thou, too, willing in the Day of Power :
    Spring from thy root, sweet flower !

DORA GREENWELL.

FEBRUARY 1st, 1842.

ONE month is past, another is begun,
    Since merry bells rang out the dying year,
And buds of rarest green began to peer,
As if impatient for a warmer sun ;
And, though the distant hills are bleak and dun,
The virgin snowdrop, like a lambent fire,
Pierces the cold earth, with its green-streaked spire ;
And, in dark woods, the wandering little one
May find a primrose.   Thus the better mind
Puts forth some flowers, escaped from Paradise,
Though faith be dim as faintest wintry skies,
And passion fierce as January wind.
O God, vouchsafe a sunbeam clear and kind,
To cheer the pining flow'ret ere it dies.

HARTLEY COLERIDGE.

A SUMMER WISH.

L IVE all thy sweet life thro',
        Sweet rose, dew-sprent;
Drop down thine evening dew
To gather it anew
When day is bright:
        I fancy thou wast meant
Chiefly to give delight.

Sing in the silent sky,
        Glad soaring bird;
Sing out thy notes on high
To sunbeam straying by
Or passing cloud;
        Heedless if thou art heard,
Sing thy full song aloud.

Oh that it were with me
        As with the flower,
Blooming on its own tree
For butterfly and bee
Its summer morns;
        That I might bloom mine hour
A rose in spite of thorns.

Oh that my work were done
        As birds' that soar
Rejoicing in the sun;
That when my time is run

And daylight too,
    I so might rest once more
Cool with refreshing dew.

CHRISTINA ROSSETTI.

OCTOBER.

FAIR leaf, so crisp and curled and yet so fair,
    Whose veinèd purples shading into bronze
    Make autumn lovely; is it hard, for once
To fall thus gently through the silent air
            And die?

Fair bird, uprising from the startled brake
    On wings that only bear thee into death,
    Is it such pain, to leave thy haunt beneath
The hazels, and of wounds that man can make
            To die?

Fair rose, yet lingering where yon topmost spray
    Climbs through the trellis o'er the garden wall,
    Is it such grief, to see thy petals fall
So fast, and, having watched them all away,
            To die?

Thus while I sit and murmur, half in dreams,
    Across the valley like a parted soul
    Shoots the white steam of travel: though its goal
Be far, it dips into the earth, and seems
            To die.

Ah then, I said, if death be only this—
  Through the dark hills a channel short and wide,
  That leads to sunshine on the other side—
Then better than the best of life it is
                        To die.
                      ARTHUR MUNBY.

THE RAINBOW.

STILL young and fine! but what is still in view
    We slight as old and soiled, though fresh and new.
How bright wert thou when Shem's admiring eye
Thy burnished flaming arch did first descry!
When Terah, Nahor, Haran, Abram, Lot,
The youthful world's grey fathers, in one knot
Did with intentive looks watch every hour
For thy new light, and trembled at each shower!
When thou dost shine, darkness looks white and fair,
Storms turn to music, clouds to smiles and air:
Rain gently spends his honey-drops, and pours
Balm on the cleft earth, milk on grass and flowers.
Bright pledge of peace and sunshine! the sure tie
Of thy Lord's hand, the object of his eye!
When I behold thee, though my light be dim,
Distant and low, I can in thine see Him
Who looks upon thee from his glorious throne,
And minds the covenant 'twixt all and One.
                    HENRY VAUGHAN.

A DROP OF DEW.

SEE how the orient dew
Shed from the bosom of the morn
Into the blowing roses,
Yet careless of its mansion new
For the clear region where 'twas born,
Round in itself incloses,
And in its little globe's extent
Frames, as it can, its native element.
How it the purple flower does slight,
Scarce touching where it lies;
But, gazing back upon the skies,
Shines with a mournful light,
Like its own tear,
Because so long divided from the sphere.
Restless it rolls and unsecure,
Trembling lest it grow impure,
Till the warm sun pities its pain,
And to the skies exhales it back again.

So the soul, that drop, that ray,
Of the clear fountain of eternal day,
Could it within the human flower be seen,
Remembering still its former height,
Shuns the sweet leaves and blossoms green,
And, recollecting its own light,
Does in its pure and circling thoughts express
The greater heaven in a heaven less.

In how coy a figure wound,
Every way it turns away ;
So the world excluding round,
Yet receiving in the day.
Dark beneath, but bright above ;
Here disdaining, there in love.
How loose and easy hence to go ;
How girt and ready to ascend ;
Moving but on a point below,
It all about does upwards bend.
Such did the manna's sacred dew distil,
White and entire, though congealed and chill ;
Congealed on earth, but does dissolving run
Into the glories of the almighty Sun.

ANDREW MARVELL.

VIRTUE.

SWEET Day, so cool, so calm, so bright,
   The bridal of the earth and sky ;
The dew shall weep thy fall to-night,
               For thou must die.

Sweet Rose, whose hue, angry and brave,
   Bids the rash gazer wipe his eye ;
Thy root is ever in its grave,
              And thou must die.

Sweet Spring, full of sweet days and roses,
  A box where sweets compacted lie ;
My music shows ye have your closes,
                    And all must die.

Only a sweet and virtuous Soul,
  Like seasoned timber, never gives ;
But, though the whole world turn to coal,
                    Then chiefly lives.

GEORGE HERBERT.

THE EVENING CLOUD.

A CLOUD lay cradled near the setting sun ;
    A gleam of crimson tinged its braided snow :
Long had I watched the glory moving on
O'er the still radiance of the lake below :
Tranquil its spirit seemed and floated slow ;
Even in its very motion there was rest ;
While every breath of eve that chanced to blow
Wafted the traveller to the beauteous West.
Emblem, methought, of the departed soul !
To whose white robe the gleam of bliss is given,
And by the breath of mercy made to roll
Right onward to the golden gates of heaven,
Where, to the eye of faith, it peaceful lies,
And tells to man his glorious destinies.

JOHN WILSON.

PARTING GLEAMS.

THE lights o'er yonder snowy range
   Shine yet, intense and tender;
Or, slowly passing, only change
   From splendour on to splendour.

Before the dying eyes of Day
   Immortal visions wander;
Dreams prescient of a purer ray,
   And morn spread still beyond her.

Lo! heavenward now those gleams expire
   In heavenly melancholy;
The barrier-mountains, peak and spire,
   Relinquishing them slowly.

Thus shine, O God, our mortal powers,
   While grief and joy refine them;
And, when in death they fade, be ours
   Thus gently to resign them.

AUBREY DE VERE.

BOOK II.

LIFE.

𝔇𝔲𝔱𝔶.

ODE TO DUTY.

STERN Daughter of the Voice of God !
　　O Duty ! if that name thou love
Who art a light to guide, a rod
　　To check the erring, and reprove ;
Thou, who art victory and law
When empty terrors overawe ;
From vain temptations dost set free,
And calm'st the weary strife of frail humanity !

There are who ask not if thine eye
　　Be on them ; who, in love and truth
Where no misgiving is, rely
　　Upon the genial sense of youth ;
Glad hearts ! without reproach or blot,
Who do thy work, and know it not :
Oh ! if through confidence misplaced
They fail, thy saving arms, dread Power, around them
　　　　cast !

Serene will be our days and bright,
   And happy will our nature be,   .
When love is an unerring light,
   And joy its own security.
And they a blissful course may hold,
Even now, who, not unwisely bold,
Live in the spirit of this creed ;
Yet seek thy firm support, according to their need.

I, loving freedom, and untried ;
   No sport of every random gust,
Yet being to myself a guide,
   Too blindly have reposed my trust ;
And oft, when in my heart was heard
Thy timely mandate, I deferred
The task, in smoother walks to stray ;
But thee I now would serve more strictly, if I may.

Through no disturbance of my soul,
   Or strong compunction in me wrought,
I supplicate for thy control ;
   But in the quietness of thought.
Me this unchartered freedom tires ;
I feel the weight of chance-desires :
My hopes no more must change their name ;
I long for a repose that ever is the same.

Stern Lawgiver ! yet thou dost wear
   The Godhead's most benignant grace ;
Nor know we any thing so fair
   As is the smile upon thy face :

Flowers laugh before thee on their beds,
And fragrance in thy footing treads ;
Thou dost preserve the stars from wrong ;
And the most ancient heavens, through Thee, are
    fresh and strong.

To humbler functions, awful Power !
    I call thee : I myself commend
Unto thy guidance from this hour ;
    Oh, let my weakness have an end !
Give unto me, made lowly wise,
The spirit of self-sacrifice ;
The confidence of reason give ;
And in the light of truth thy bondman let me live !

WILLIAM WORDSWORTH.

THE RIGHT MUST WIN.

OH it is hard to work for God,
    To rise and take his part
Upon this battle-field of earth,
    And not sometimes lose heart !

He hides himself so wondrously,
    As though there were no God ;
He is least seen when all the powers
    Of ill are most abroad.

Or He deserts us at the hour
    The fight is all but lost ;

And seems to leave us to ourselves
    Just when we need Him most.

It is not so, but so it looks ;
    And we lose courage then ;
And doubts will come if God hath kept
    His promises to men.

Ah ! God is other than we think ;
    His ways are far above,
Far beyond reason's height, and reached
    Only by child-like love.

The look, the fashion of God's ways,
    Love's lifelong study are ;
She can be bold, and guess, and act,
    When reason would not dare.

Thrice blest is he to whom is given
    The instinct that can tell
That God is on the field when He
    Is most invisible.

Blest, too, is he who can divine
    Where real right doth lie,
And dares to take the side that seems
    Wrong to man's blindfold eye.

Then learn to scorn the praise of men,
    And learn to lose with God ;
For Jesus won the world through shame,
    And beckons thee his road.

For right is right, since God is God ;
And right the day must win ;
To doubt would be disloyalty,
To falter would be sin.

FREDERICK WILLIAM FABER.

THE MANLY LIFE.

THRICE happy he whose name is writ above,
And doeth good though gaining infamy;
Requiteth evil turns with hearty love,
And recks not what befalls him outwardly:
Whose worth is in himself, and only bliss
In his pure conscience that doth nought amiss.

Who placeth pleasure in his purgèd soul,
And virtuous life his treasure doth esteem ;
Who can his passions master and control,
And that true lordly manliness doth deem ;
Who from this world himself hath clearly quit,
Counts nought his own but what lives in his sprite.

So, when his sprite from this vain world shall flit,
It bears all with it whatsoe'er was dear
Unto itself, passing in easy fit,
As kindly ripened corn comes out of th' ear.
Thus, mindless of what idle men will say,
He takes his own and stilly goes his way.

HENRY MORE.

ON HIS BEING ARRIVED TO THE AGE OF TWENTY-THREE.

HOW soon hath Time, the subtle thief of youth,
    Stol'n on his wing my three-and-twentieth year!
My hasting days fly on with full career,
But my late spring no bud or blossom show'th.
Perhaps my semblance might deceive the truth
That I to manhood am arrived so near,
And inward ripeness doth much less appear,
That some more timely-happy spirits indu'th.
Yet, be it less or more, or soon or slow,
It shall be still in strictest measure even
'To that same lot, however mean or high,
Toward which Time leads me, and the will of Heaven
All is, if I have grace to use it so,
 As ever in my great task-master's eye.

                                JOHN MILTON.

ON HIS BLINDNESS.

WHEN I consider how my light is spent
    Ere half my days, in this dark world and wide,
And that one talent which is death to hide,
Lodged with me useless, though my soul more bent
To serve therewith my Maker, and present
My true account, lest He returning chide;

'Doth God exact day labour, light denied?'
I fondly ask : but Patience, to prevent
That murmur, soon replies, 'God doth not need
Either man's work, or his own gifts ; who best
Bear his mild yoke, they serve him best; his state
Is kingly; thousands at his bidding speed,
And post o'er land and ocean without rest :—
They also serve who only stand and wait.'

JOHN MILTON.

LONDON, 1802.

MILTON ! thou should'st be living at this hour :
    England hath need of thee : she is a fen
Of stagnant waters : altar, sword, and pen,
Fireside, the heroic wealth of hall and bower,
Have forfeited their ancient English dower
Of inward happiness.   We are selfish men :
Oh raise us up, return to us again,
And give us manners, virtue, freedom, power.
Thy soul was like a star, and dwelt apart :
Thou hadst a voice whose sound was like the sea :
Pure as the naked heavens, majestic, free,
So didst thou travel on life's common way,
In cheerful godliness ; and yet thy heart
The lowliest duties on herself did lay.

WILLIAM WORDSWORTH.

NOT MADE IN VAIN.

L ET me not deem that I was made in vain,
　　Or that my being was an accident
Which fate, in working its sublime intent,
Not wished to be—to hinder would not deign.
Each drop uncounted in a storm of rain
Hath its own mission, and is duly sent
To its own leaf or blade, not idly spent
'Mid myriad dimples on the shipless main.
The very shadow of an insect's wing,
For which the violet cared not while it stayed,
Yet felt the lighter for its vanishing,
Proved that the sun was shining, by its shade.
Then can a drop of the eternal spring,
Shadow of living lights, in vain be made?

　　　　　　　　　　HARTLEY COLERIDGE.

SELF-DEPENDENCE.

W EARY of myself, and sick of asking
　　What I am, and what I ought to be,
At the vessel's prow I stand, which bears me
Forwards, forwards, o'er the star-lit sea.

And a look of passionate desire
O'er the sea and to the stars I send:
'Ye who from my childhood up have calmed me,
Calm me, ah, compose me to the end!

'Ah, once more,' I cried, 'ye stars, ye waters,
On my heart your mighty charm renew!
Still, still let me, as I gaze upon you,
Feel my soul becoming vast like you!'

From the intense, clear, star-sown vault of heaven,
Over the lit sea's unquiet way,
In the rustling night air came the answer—
'Would'st thou *be* as they are? *Live* as they!

'Unaffrighted by the silence round them,
Undistracted by the sights they see,   .
These demand not that the things without them
Yield them love, amusement, sympathy.

'And with joy the stars perform their shining,
And the sea its long moon-silvered roll.
Why?—self-poised they live, nor pine with noting
All the fever of some differing soul.

'Bounded by themselves and unregardful
In what state God's other works may be,
In their own tasks all their powers pouring,
These attain the mighty life you see.'

———

O air-born voice! long since, severely clear,
A cry like thine in mine own heart I hear:
'Resolve to be thyself! and know, that he
Who finds himself, loses his misery!'

MATTHEW ARNOLD.

MORALITY.

WE cannot kindle when we will
        The fire which in the heart resides,
The spirit bloweth and is still,
        In mystery our soul abides :
But tasks in hours of insight willed
Can be through hours of gloom fulfilled.

With aching hands and bleeding feet
·   We dig and heap, lay stone on stone;
We bear the burden and the heat
        Of the long day, and wish 'twere done.
Not till the hours of light return
All we have built do we discern.

Then, when the clouds are off the soul,
        When thou dost bask in Nature's eye,
Ask how *she* viewed thy self-control,
        Thy struggling tasked morality—
Nature, whose free, light, cheerful air,
Oft made thee, in thy gloom, despair.

And she, whose censure thou dost dread,
        Whose eye thou wast afraid to seek,
See, on her face a glow is spread,
        A strong emotion on her cheek !
' Ah, child !' she cries, ' that strife divine—
Whence was it, for it is not mine ?

'There is no effort on *my* brow—
   I do not strive, I do not weep;
I rush with the swift spheres, and glow
   In joy, and, when I will, I sleep.
Yet that severe, that earnest air,
I saw, I felt it once—but where?

'I knew not yet the gauge of time,
   Nor wore the manacles of space;
I felt it in some other clime—
   I saw it in some other place.
'Twas when the heavenly house I trod,
And lay upon the breast of God.'

MATTHEW ARNOLD.

ALL SAINTS.

ONE feast, of holy days the crest,
   I, though no churchman, love to keep;
All-Saints,—the unknown good that rest
   In God's still memory folded deep.
The bravely dumb that did their deed,
   And scorned to blot it with a name,
Men of the plain heroic breed,
   That loved Heaven's silence more than fame.

Such lived not in the past alone,
   But thread to-day the unheeding street,
And stairs to Sin and Famine known
   Sing with the welcome of their feet;

The den they enter grows a shrine,
The grimy sash an oriel burns,
Their cup of water warms like wine,
Their speech is filled from heavenly urns.

About their brows to me appears
An aureole traced in tenderest light,
The rainbow-gleam of smiles through tears
In dying eyes, by them made bright,
Of souls that shivered on the edge
Of that chill ford repassed no more,
And in their mercy felt the pledge
And sweetness of the farther shore.

JAMES RUSSELL LOWELL.

GOOD LIFE, LONG LIFE.

IT is not growing like a tree,
In bulk, doth make men better be;
Or standing long, an oak, three hundred year,
To fall a log at last, dry, bald, and sere.
A lily of a day
Is fairer far in May,
Although it fall and die that night;
It was the plant and flower of light.
In small proportions we just beauties see,
And in short measures life may perfect be.

BEN JONSON.

I WILL ARISE.

WHO, toiling on the weary round of life,
But feels sometimes,—when all the way is dark,
And mists of sense and clouds of weariness
Close round him, and before him stretches out
Life's journey, an interminable moor,
And all the future like a barren road
Through the long waste of years,—lo, suddenly
The mists rise like a curtain, and he knows
The presence of the everlasting hills ;
Height after height, peak after peak revealed ;
The filmy downward cataract, the chill
Unearthly whiteness of untrodden snows ;
And, somewhere in the space 'twixt them and heaven,
The eagle circling sunward ! So his soul
Knows it must quit the smooth ignoble paths,
To tread on rugged heights, scale precipices,
Sway on the trembling bridge which spans the foam,
Creep where the thund'rous avalanche sweeps, the bolt
Shivers the patient rocks, feel the mad winds
Rush round him like a chaos. If he know
Something of new-born joy, yet is it dashed
With craven chills of fear ; fain would he climb,
But looking upward dare not. Then, perchance,
Shines out athwart the gathered clouds of sense
The great sun's awful face ; and lo ! the snows
Which erewhile showed so cold, so deadly calm,
Redden with a blush of life ; the light reveals,
High on the scarpèd cliffs, the giddy paths

Where men have trodden and lived.   Then his whole
   soul,
Stirred to the deeps of passionate utterance,
Cries loud, ' I will arise, I will arise ;'
And, while the sun shines, climbs.   Happy are they
On whom the clouds descend not to blot out
What glimpse they had of heaven.   Some men there be
Who, toiling through the mist, ne'er see the sun,
And live a slavish life and know it not,
And die, poor souls ! i' the plain.   Others there be
Who, when in some chance ray they fain would rise,
The envious clouds shut out the face of heaven,
And they may mount no higher.   Fewer still
Girding their loins, without a glance behind,
Mount ever upward in that mystical light,
Above the earth's gross humours, till the air
Grows purer, and the paths which seemed so steep
Are smoothed before them and they tread the snows,
Where other footsteps few and rare shall come
In the efflux of the ages—storm and cloud
Left far beneath ; God shining overhead ;
And round them all the changeless calm of Heaven.
SONGS OF TWO WORLDS.

FLOWERS WITHOUT FRUIT.

PRUNE thou thy words, the thoughts control
    That o'er thee swell and throng ;
They will condense within thy soul,
    And change to purpose strong.

But he who lets his feelings run
　In soft luxurious flow,
Shrinks when hard service must be done,
　And faints at every woe.

Faith's meanest deed more favour bears,
　Where hearts and wills are weighed,
Than brightest transports, choicest prayers,
　Which bloom their hour and fade.

JOHN HENRY NEWMAN.

WORK AND CONTEMPLATION.

THE woman singeth at her spinning-wheel
　A pleasant chant, ballad or barcarole ;
She thinketh of her song, upon the whole,
Far more than of her flax ; and yet the reel
Is full, and artfully her fingers feel
With quick adjustment, provident control,
The lines, too subtly twisted to unroll,
Out to a perfect thread.　I hence appeal
To the dear Christian Church—that we may do
Our Father's business in these temples mirk,
Thus swift and steadfast, thus intent and strong ;
While thus, apart from toil, our souls pursue
Some high, calm, spheric tune, and prove our work
The better for the sweetness of our song.

ELIZABETH BARRETT BROWNING.

G

A CHRISTMAS CAROL.

IT chanced upon the merry merry Christmas eve,
   I went sighing past the church across the moor-
      land dreary—
'Oh ! never sin and want and woe this earth will leave,
  And the bells but mock the wailing round, they sing
     so cheery.
How long, O Lord ! how long before Thou come again?
  Still in cellar, and in garret, and on moorland dreary
The orphans moan, and widows weep, and poor men
    toil in vain,
  Till earth is sick of hope deferred, though Christmas
    bells be cheery.'

Then arose a joyous clamour from the wild-fowl on
    the mere,
  Beneath the stars, across the snow, like clear
    bells ringing,
And a voice within cried—'Listen ! Christmas carols
    even here !
  Though thou be dumb, yet o'er their work the
    stars and snows are singing.
Blind ! I live, I love, I reign ; and all the nations
    through
  With the thunder of my judgments even now are
    ringing ;
   thou fulfil thy work but as yon wild-fowl do,
  Thou wilt heed no less the wailing, yet hear thro' it
    angels singing.'

CHARLES KINGSLEY.

EVERY DAY.

LET us not teach and preach so much,
　　But cherish, rather than profess ;
Be careful how the thoughts we touch
　　Of God, and Love, and Holiness,—

A charm, most spiritual, faint,
　　And delicate, forsakes the breast,
Bird-like, when it perceives the taint
　　Of prying breath upon its nest.

Using, enjoying, let us live;
　　Set here to grow, what should we do
But take what soil and climate give ?
　　For thence must come our sap and hue: .

Blooming as sweetly as we may,
　　Nor beckon comers, nor debar ;
Let them take balm or gall away,
　　According as their natures are :

Look straight at all things from the soul,
　　But boast not much to understand ;
Make each new action sound and whole,
　　Then leave it in its place unscanned :

Be true, devoid of aim or care;
　　Nor posture, nor antagonize :
Know well that clouds of this our air
　　But seem to wrap the mighty skies.

Search starry mysteries overhead,
  Where wonders gleam ; yet bear in mind
That Earth's our planet, firm to tread,
  Nor in the star-dance left behind :

For nothing is withheld, be sure,
  Our being needed to have shown ;
The far was meant to be obscure,
  The near was placed so to be known.

Cast we no astrologic scheme
  To map the course we must pursue ;
But use the lights whene'er they beam,
  And every trusty landmark too.

The Future let us not permit
  To choke us in its shadow's clasp ;
It cannot touch us, nor we it ;
  The present moment's in our grasp.

Soul severed from the truth is sin ;
  The dark and dizzy gulf is doubt ;
Truth never moves,—unmoved therein,
  Our road is straight and firm throughout.

This road for ever doth abide.
  The universe, if fate so call,
May sink away on either side ;
  But This and GOD at once shall fall.

                            WILLIAM ALLINGHAM.

PUSILLANIMITY.

'I have need to be baptized of Thee, and comest Thou to me ?'

HOW didst thou start, Thou Holy Baptist, bid
   To pour repentance on the Sinless Brow !
Then all thy meekness, from thy hearers hid
   Beneath the Ascetic's port and Preacher's fire,
Flowed forth, and with a pang thou didst desire
   He might be chief, not thou.

And so on us, at whiles, it falls to claim
   Powers that we dread, or dare some forward part;
Nor must we shrink as cravens from the blame
   Of pride, in common eyes, or purpose deep ;
But with pure thoughts look up to God, and keep
   Our secret in our heart.

JOHN HENRY NEWMAN

SENSITIVENESS.

TIME was, I shrank from what was right,
   From fear of what was wrong;
I would not brave the sacred fight,
   Because the foe was strong.

But now I cast that finer sense
   And sorer shame aside ;
Such dread of sin was indolence,
   Such aim at heaven was pride.

So, when my Saviour calls, I rise,
  And calmly do my best ;
Leaving to Him, with silent eyes
  Of hope and fear, the rest.

I step, I mount where He has led ;
  Men count my haltings o'er ;—
I know them ; yet, though self I dread,
  I love his precept more.

                JOHN HENRY NEWMAN.

Discipline.

SEMITA JUSTORUM.

WHEN I look back upon my former race,
 Seasons I see, at which the Inward Ray
More brightly burned, or guided some new way;
Truth, in its wealthier scene and nobler space,
Given for my eye to range, and feet to trace:
And next I mark, 'twas trial did convey,
Or grief, or pain, or strange eventful day,
To my tormented soul such larger grace.
So now, whene'er, in journeying on, I feel
The shadow of the Providential Hand,
Deep breathless stirrings shoot across my breast,
Searching to know what He will now reveal,
What sin uncloak, what stricter rule command,
And girding me to work his full behest.

JOHN HENRY NEWMAN.

MAN.

WEIGHING the steadfastness and state
    Of some mean things which here below
    reside,
Where birds, like watchful clocks, the noiseless date
    And intercourse of times divide,
Where bees at night get home and hive, and flowers,
    Early as well as late,
Rise with the sun, and set in the same bowers;

    I would, said I, my God would give
The staidness of these things to man ! for these
To his divine appointments ever cleave,
    And no new business breaks their peace :
The birds nor sow nor reap, yet sup and dine ;
    The flowers without clothes live,
Yet Solomon was never dressed so fine.

    Man hath still either toys or care :
He hath no root, nor to one place is tied,
But, ever restless and irregular,
    About this earth doth run and ride.
He knows he hath a home, but scarce knows where :
    He says it is so far
That he hath quite forgot how to go there.

    He knocks at all doors, strays and roams ;
Nay, hath not so much wit as some stones have,
Which, in the darkest nights, point to their homes,
    By some hid sense their Maker gave.

Man is the shuttle, to whose winding quest
And passage through these looms
God ordered motion, but ordained no rest.

HENRY VAUGHAN.

THE PULLEY.

WHEN God at first made man,
Having a glass of blessings standing by;
Let us, said He, pour on him all we can :
Let the world's riches which dispersèd lie
Contract into a span.

So strength first made a way,
Then beauty flowed, then wisdom, honour, pleasure :
When almost all was out, God made a stay,
Perceiving that alone, of all his treasure,
Rest in the bottom lay.

For if I should, said He,
Bestow this jewel also on my creature,
He would adore my gifts, instead of Me,
And rest in Nature, not the God of Nature,—
So both should losers be.

Yet let him keep the rest,
But keep them with repining restlessness :
Let him be rich and weary, that at least
If goodness lead him not, yet weariness
May toss him to my breast.

GEORGE HERBERT.

THE COLLAR.

I STRUCK the board, and cried, 'No more !
    I will abroad.
What! shall I ever sigh and pine?
My lines and life are free, free as the road,
Loose as the wind, as large as store.
      Shall I be still in suit?
Have I no harvest but a thorn
To let me blood, and not restore
What I have lost with cordial fruit?
      Sure there was wine,
Before my sighs did dry it: there was corn
      Before my tears did drown it.
  Is the year only lost to me?
      Have I no bays to crown it?
No flowers, no garlands gay?   All blasted?
      All wasted?
  Not so, my heart; but there is fruit,
      And thou hast hands.
    Recover all thy sigh-blown age
On double pleasures.   Leave thy cold dispute
Of what is fit, and not.   Forsake thy cage,
      Thy rope of sands
Which petty thoughts have made, and made to thee
    Good cable, to enforce and draw
      And be thy law,
While thou didst wink and wouldst not see.
      Away! take heed!
      I will abroad.

Call in thy death's-head there !   Tie up thy fears !
He that forbears
To suit and serve his need
Deserves his load.'
But as I raved, and grew more fierce and wild
At every word,
Methought I heard one calling, ' Child !'
And I replied, ' My Lord !'

GEORGE HERBERT.

JOY IN SORROW.

'As sorrowful, yet always rejoicing.'

GIVE me thy joy in sorrow, gracious Lord,
And sorrow's self shall like to joy appear !
Although the world should waver in its sphere
I tremble not, if Thou thy peace afford.
But, Thou withdrawn, I am but as a chord
That vibrates to the pulse of hope and fear ;
Nor rest I more than harps which to the air
Must answer when we place their tuneful board
Against the blast, which thrill unmeaning woe
Even in their sweetness.   So no earthly wing
E'er sweeps me but to sadden.   Oh, place Thou
My heart beyond the world's sad vibrating :
And where but in Thyself?   Oh, circle me,
That I may feel no touches save of Thee.

CHAUNCY HARE TOWNSHEND.

FIVE SONNETS FROM 'WITHIN AND WITHOUT.'

I.

GO thou into thy closet; shut thy door;
    And pray to Him in secret: He will hear.
But think not thou, by one wild bound, to clear
The numberless ascensions, more and more,
Of starry stairs that must be climbed, before
Thou comest to the Father's likeness near;
And bendest down to kiss the feet so dear
That, step by step, their mounting flights passed o'er.
Be thou content if on thy weary need
There falls a sense of showers and of the spring;
A hope, that makes it possible to fling
Sickness aside, and go and do the deed;
For highest aspiration will not lead
Unto the calm beyond all questioning.

II.

Hark, hark, a voice amid the quiet intense!
It is thy Duty waiting thee without.
Rise from thy knees in hope, the half of doubt;
A hand doth pull thee—it is Providence.
Open thy door straightway, and get thee hence;
Go forth into the tumult and the shout;
Work, love, with workers, lovers, all about:
Of noise alone is born the inward sense
Of silence; and from action springs alone
The inward knowledge of true love and faith.

Then, weary, go thou back with failing breath,
And in thy chamber make thy prayer and moan :
One day upon *his* bosom, all thine own,
Thou shalt lie still, embraced in holy death.

III.

And weep not, though the Beautiful decay
Within thy heart, as daily in thine eyes ;
Thy heart must have its autumn, its pale skies,
Leading, mayhap, to winter's dim dismay.
Yet doubt not. Beauty doth not pass away ;
Her form departs not, though her body dies.
Secure beneath the earth the snowdrop lies,
Waiting the spring's young resurrection-day,
Through the kind nurture of the winter cold.
Nor seek thou by vain effort to revive
The summer time, when roses were alive ;
Do thou thy work—be willing to be old :
Thy sorrow is the husk that doth enfold
A gorgeous June for which thou need'st not strive.

IV.

And should the twilight darken into night,
And sorrow grow to anguish, be thou strong ;
Thou art in God, and nothing can go wrong
Which a fresh life-pulse cannot set aright.
That thou dost know the darkness, proves the light.
Weep if thou wilt, but weep not all too long ;
Or weep and work, for work will lead to song.
But search thy heart, if hid from all thy sight

There lie no cause for beauty's slow decay;
If for completeness and diviner youth,
And not for very love, thou seek'st the truth ;
If thou hast learned to give thyself away
For love's own self, not for thyself, I say :
Were God's love less, the world were lost, in sooth.

v.

And do not fear to hope.   Can poet's brain
More than the father's heart rich good invent?
Each time we smell the autumn's dying scent,
We know the primrose time will come again ;
Not more we hope, nor less would soothe our pain.
Be bounteous in thy faith, for not misspent
Is confidence unto the Father lent :
Thy need is sown and rooted for his rain.
His thoughts are as thine own ; nor are his ways
Other than thine, but by their loftier sense
Of beauty infinite and love intense.
Work on.   One day, beyond all thoughts of praise,
A sunny joy will crown thee with its rays ;
Nor other than thy need, thy recompense.

GEORGE MacDONALD.

A DAY'S RELEASE.

DAY after day, until to-day,
    Imaged its fellows gone before,
The same dull task, the weary way,
    The weakness pardoned o'er and o'er,

The thwarted thirst, too faintly felt,
  For joy's well-nigh forgotten life,
The restless heart, which, when I knelt,
  Made of my worship barren strife.

Ah, whence to-day's so sweet release;
  This clearance light of all my care,
This conscience free, this fertile peace,
  These softly-folded wings of prayer;

This calm and more than conquering love,
  With which the tempter dares not cope;
This joy that lifts no glance above,
  For faith too sure, too sweet for hope?

O, happy time, too happy change,
  It will not live, though fondly nursed!
Full soon this day will seem as strange
  As now the dark which seems dispersed.

COVENTRY PATMORE.

AGAINST TEARS.

THIS world is all too sad for tears,
  I would not weep, not I,
But smile along my life's short road,
  Until I, smiling, die.

The little flowers breathe sweetness out
    Through all the dewy night;
Should I more churlish be than they,
    And 'plain for constant light?

Not so, not so, no load of woe
    Need bring despairing frown;
For while we bear it, we can bear,
    Past that, we lay it down.

SARAH WILLIAMS.

WEARINESS.

ART thou already weary of the way?
    Thou who hast yet but half the way gone o'er:
Get up, and lift thy burden; lo! before
Thy feet the road goes stretching far away.
If thou already faint who hast but come
Through half thy pilgrimage, with fellows gay,
Love, youth, and hope, under the rosy bloom
And temperate airs of early breaking day,—
Look yonder, how the heavens stoop and gloom.
There cease the trees to shade, the flowers to spring,
And the angels leave thee. What wilt thou become
Through yon drear stretch of dismal wandering,
Lonely and dark?—I shall take courage, friend,
For comes not every step more near the end?

FRANCES ANNE KEMBLE.

SONNET.

MOURNER, that dost deserve thy mournfulness,
 Call thyself punished, call the earth thy hell ;
Say 'God is angry, and I earned it well ;
I would not have Him smile and not redress.'
Say this, and straightway all thy grief grows less.
 'God rules at least, I find, as prophets tell,
 And proves it in this prison.' Straight thy cell
Smiles with an unsuspected loveliness.
—'A prison—and yet, from door and window-bar,
 I catch a thousand breaths of his sweet air ;
 Even to me his days and nights are fair ;
He shows me many a flower, and many a star ;
And though I mourn, and He is very far,
 He does not kill the hope that reaches there.'

ANONYMOUS.

A DREAM OF THE CROSS.

DREAMING I slept. Three crosses stood
 High in the gloomy air ;
One bore a thief, and one the Good :
 The third cross waited bare.

A soldier coming to the place,
 Would hang me on the third :
Mine eyes they sought the master's face,
 My will the master's word.

H

He bent his head; I took the sign
   And gave the error way;
Gesture nor look nor word of mine
   The secret should betray.

A moment from the cross's foot
   He turned, and left me there,
Waiting till that grim tree for fruit
   My dying form should bear.

Up rose the steaming mists of doubt,
   And chilled both heart and brain;
They shut the world of vision out,
   And fear saw only pain.

'Ah me, my hands! the hammer's blow!
   The nails that rend and pierce!
The shock may stun, but slow and slow
   The torture will grow fierce.

'Alas, the awful fight with death!
   The hours to hang and die!
The thirsting gasp for common breath!
   The weakness that would cry!'

My soul returned, 'A faintness soon
   Will shroud thee in its fold;
The hours will bring the fearful noon;
   'Twill pass—and thou art cold.

' 'Tis his to care that thou endure,
  To curb or loose the pain ;
With bleeding hands hang on thy cure—
  It shall not be in vain.'

But ah ! the will, which thus could quail,
  Might yield—oh, horror drear !
Then more than love, the fear to fail
  Kept down the other fear.

I stood, nor moved. But inward strife
  The bonds of slumber broke :
Oh ! had I fled, and lost the life
  Of which the master spoke ?

GEORGE MACDONALD.

ISOLATION.

M AN dwells apart, though not alone ;
      He walks among his peers unread ;
The best of thoughts which he hath known,
  For lack of listeners are not said.

Yet dreaming on earth's clustered isles,
  He saith, ' They dwell not lone like men,'
Forgetful that their sunflecked smiles
  Flash far beyond each other's ken.

H 2

He looks on God's eternal suns
   That sprinkle the celestial blue,
And saith, 'Ah! happy shining ones,
   I would that men were grouped like you!'

Yet this is sure, the loveliest star
   That clustered with its peers we see,
Only because from us so far
   Doth near its fellows seem to be.

                         JEAN INGELOW.

EXAGGERATION.

WE overstate the ills of life, and take
     Imagination (given us to bring down
The choirs of singing angels overshone
By God's clear glory) down our earth to rake
The dismal snows instead, flake following flake,
To cover all the corn; we walk upon
The shadow of hills across a level thrown,
And pant like climbers; near the alderbrake
We sigh so loud, the nightingale within
Refuses to sing loud, as else she would.
O brothers, let us leave the shame and sin
Of taking vainly, in a plaintive mood,
The holy name of GRIEF!—holy herein,
That by the grief of ONE came all our good.

          ELIZABETH BARRETT BROWNING.

FINITE AND INFINITE.

THE wind sounds only in opposing straits,
   The sea, beside the shore ; man's spirit rends
Its quiet only up against the ends
Of wants and oppositions, loves and hates,
Where, worked and worn by passionate debates,
And losing by the loss it apprehends,
The flesh rocks round and every breath it sends
Is ravelled to a sigh.   All tortured states
Suppose a straitened place.   Jehovah Lord,
Make room for rest around me ! out of sight
Now float me, of the vexing land abhorred,
Till in deep calms of space my soul may right
Her nature, shoot large sail on lengthening cord,
And rush exultant on the Infinite.

ELIZABETH BARRETT BROWNING.

THE MESSENGER.

A MESSENGER that stood beside my bed,
   In words of clear and cruel import said,
(And yet methought the tone was less unkind,)
'I bring thee pain of body and of mind.

'Each gift of each must pay a toll to me ;
Nor flight, nor force, nor suit can set thee free ;
Until my brother come, I say not when :
Affliction is my name, unloved of men.'

I swooned, then, bursting up in talk deranged,
Shattered to tears; while he stood by unchanged.
I held my peace, my heart with courage burned,
And to his cold touch one faint sigh returned.

Undreamt-of wings he lifted, 'For awhile
I vanish.   Never be afraid to smile
Lest I waylay thee : curse me not ; nay, love ;
That I may bring thee tidings from above.'

And often since, by day or night, descends
The face obdurate ; now almost a friend's.
Oh ! quite to Faith ; but Frailty's lips not dare
The word.   To both this angel taught a prayer.

'Lord God, thy servant, wounded and bereft,
Feels Thee upon his right hand and his left ;
Hath joy in grief, and still by losing gains ;—
All this is gone, yet all myself remains !'

WILLIAM ALLINGHAM.

Penitence.

LEVAVI OCULOS.

IN trouble for my sin, I cried to God,—
To the Great God who dwelleth in the deeps.
The deeps return not any voice or sign.

But with my soul I know Thee, O Great God;
The soul Thou givest knoweth Thee, Great God;
And with my soul I sorrow for my sin.

Full sure I am there is no joy in sin;
Joy-scented peace is trampled under foot,
Like a white growing blossom into mud.

Sin is established subtly in the heart
As a disease; like a magician foul
Ruleth the better thoughts against their will.

Only the rays of God can cure the heart,
Purge it of evil: there's no other way
Except to turn with the whole heart to God.

In heavenly sunlight live no shades of fear;
The soul there, busy or at rest, hath peace ;
And music floweth from the various world.

The Lord is great and good, and is our God.
There needeth not a word but only these;
Our God is good, our God is great.   'Tis well!

All things are ever God's ; the shows of things
Are of man's fantasy, and warped with sin ;
God, and the things of God, immutable.

O great good God, my pray'r is to neglect
The shows of fantasy, and turn myself
To thy unfenced, unmeasured warmth and light !

Then were all shows of things a part of truth :
Then were my soul, if busy or at rest,
Residing in the house of perfect peace !

                            WILLIAM ALLINGHAM.

PENITENCE.

BECAUSE I knew not when my life was good
     And when there was a light upon my path,
But turned my soul perversely to the dark—
          O Lord, I do repent.

Because I held upon my selfish road,
And left my brother wounded by the way,
And called ambition duty, and pressed on—
          O Lord, I do repent.

Because I spent the strength Thou gavest me
In struggle which Thou never didst ordain,
And have but dregs of life to offer Thee—
    O Lord, I do repent.

Because I chose the thorns, and 'plained for flowers,
And pressed the sword-points down upon my heart,
And moaned that they did hurt me, like a child—
    O Lord, I do repent.

Because I struck at others in my pain,
Like some wild beast that, wounded, turns at bay,
And rends the innocent earth he stands upon—
    O Lord, I do repent.

Because I was impatient, would not wait,
But thrust mine impious hand across thy threads,
And marred the pattern drawn out for my life—
    O Lord, I do repent.

Because I called good evil, evil good,
And thought I, ignorant, knew many things,
And deemed my weight of folly weight of wit—
    O Lord, I do repent.

Because Thou hast borne with me all this while,
Hast smitten me with love until I weep,
Hast called me, as a mother calls her child—
    O Lord, I do repent.

SARAH WILLIAMS.

SIN.

L ORD, with what care hast Thou begirt us round!
   Parents first season us ; then schoolmasters
Deliver us to laws ; they send us bound
To rules of reason, holy messengers ;
Pulpits and Sundays, sorrow dogging sin,
   Afflictions sorted, anguish of all sizes,
   Fine nets and stratagems to catch us in,
Bibles laid open, millions of surprises,
Blessings beforehand, ties of gratefulness,
   The sound of glory ringing in our ears ;
Without, our shame ; within, our consciences ;
   Angels and grace, eternal hopes and fears.
Yet all these fences and their whole array
One cunning bosom-sin blows quite away.

GEORGE HERBERT.

IN THE SHADOWS.

O THOU of purer eyes than to behold
   Uncleanness ! sift my soul, removing all
   Strange thoughts, imaginings fantastical,
Iniquitous allurements manifold.
Make it a spiritual ark, abode
   Severely sacred, perfumed, sanctified,
   Wherein the Prince of Purities may abide—
The holy and eternal Spirit of God.

The gross, adhesive loathsomeness of sin
  Give me to see. Yet, oh far more, far more,
  That beautiful purity which the saints adore,
In a consummate Paradise within
  The veil,—O Lord, upon my soul bestow,
  An earnest of that purity here below.

DAVID GRAY.

DESIRE.

THOU, who dost dwell alone—
  Thou, who dost know thine own—
Thou, to whom all are known
From the cradle to the grave—
  Save, oh, save!
From the world's temptations,
  From tribulations;
From that fierce anguish
Wherein we languish;
From that torpor deep
Wherein we lie asleep,
Heavy as death, cold as the grave;
  Save, oh, save!

When the Soul, growing clearer,
. Sees God no nearer:
When the Soul, mounting higher,
  To God comes no nigher:
But the arch-fiend Pride
Mounts at her side,

Foiling her high emprise,
Sealing her eagle eyes,
And, when she fain would soar
Makes idols to adore ;
Changing the pure emotion
Of her high devotion
To a skin-deep sense
Of her own eloquence ;
Strong to deceive, strong to enslave-
        Save, oh, save !

From the ingrained fashion
Of this earthly nature
That mars thy creature ;
From grief, that is but passion ;
From mirth, that is but feigning ;
From tears, that bring no healing ;
From wild and weak complaining ;
    Thine old strength revealing,
        Save, oh, save !

From doubt, where all is double :
Where wise men are not strong :
Where comfort turns to trouble :
Where just men suffer wrong :
Where sorrow treads on joy :
Where sweet things soonest cloy :
Where faiths are built on dust :
Where love is half mistrust,
Hungry, and barren, and sharp as the sea ;
        Oh, set us free !

O let the false dream fly
Where our sick souls do lie
  Tossing continually.
O where thy voice doth come
  Let all doubts be dumb :
  Let all words be mild :
  All strifes be reconciled :
  All pains beguiled.
Light bring no blindness ;
Love no unkindness ;
Knowledge no ruin ;
Fear no undoing.
From the cradle to the grave,
    Save, oh, save !

MATTHEW ARNOLD.

BLOTTED PAGES.

EACH day a page is of my being's book,
    And what I do is what I write therein ;
And often do I make great blots of sin ;
And seldom proves the writing much akin
To what, before 'twas writ, I undertook.

I turn a fresh leaf daily, and renew
My hopes of *now at last a nobler page.*
But presently in something I engage
That looks but poorly in a calm review,
And leaves my future a mean heritage.

So leaf on leaf, once clean, is turned and gone,
And the dark spots shine through, and I grow sad,
And blush, and frown, and sigh. And if I had
A million pages yet to write upon,
Perhaps the millionth would be just as bad.

What shall I do?—some new leaves even yet
May be before me. And perhaps I may
Write, even yet, some not ignoble day.
Alas! I do not know :—I cannot say.
What is it to feel living?—I forget.

HENRY SEPTIMUS SUTTON.

LOSS.

GRIEVE not much for loss of wealth,
  Loss of friends, or loss of fame,
Loss of years, or loss of health ;
  Answer, hast thou lost the shame
Whose early tremor once could flush
Thy cheek, and make thine eyes to gush,
And send thy spirit, sad and sore,
To kneel with face upon the floor,   .
Burdened with consciousness of sin?
Art thou cold and hard within,—
Sometimes looking back surprised
On thy old mood, scarce recognized,
As on a picture of thy face
In blooming childhood's transient grace ?

Then hast thou cause for grief; and most
In seldom missing what is lost.
With the loss of Yesterday,
   Thou hast lost To-day, To-morrow,—
All thou might'st have been.   O pray
   (If pray thou canst) for poignant sorrow.

WILLIAM ALLINGHAM.

FATHER, I HAVE SINNED.

O FATHER, I have sinned !   I have done
    The thing I thought I never more should do.
My days were set before me, light all through ;
But I have made them dark, alas ! too true,
And drawn dense clouds between me and my sun.

Forgive me not, for grievous is my sin ;
Yea very deep and dark.   Alas ! I see
Such blackness in it that I may not be
Forgiven of myself ; how then of Thee ?
Vile, vile without ! black, utter black within !

If my shut eyes should dare their lids to part,
I know how they must quail beneath the blaze
Of thy love's greatness.   No ! I dare not raise
One prayer, to look aloft, lest it should gaze
On such forgiveness as would break my heart.

HENRY SEPTIMUS SUTTON.

TO-MORROW.

L ORD, what am I, that, with unceasing care,
　　Thou didst seek after me, that thou didst wait,
Wet with unhealthy dews, before my gate,
And pass the gloomy nights of winter there ?
Oh, strange delusion !—that I did not greet
Thy blest approach ; and oh, to Heaven how lost,
If my ingratitude's unkindly frost
Has chilled the bleeding wounds upon thy feet.
How oft my guardian angel gently cried,
' Soul, from thy casement look, and thou shalt see
How He persists to knock and wait for thee !'
And oh ! how often to that voice of sorrow,
' To-morrow we will open,' I replied ;
And, when the morrow came, I answered still,
　' To-morrow.'

HENRY WADSWORTH LONGFELLOW
(*from* LOPE DE VEGA).

MEA CULPA.

A T me one night the angry moon,
　　Suspended to a rim of cloud,
Glared through the courses of the wind.
Suddenly then my spirit bowed
And shrunk into a fearful swoon
That made me deaf and blind.

We sinned—we sin—is that a dream?
We wake—there is no voice nor stir;
Sin and repent from day to day,
As though some reeking murderer
Should dip his hand in a running stream,
And lightly go his way.

Embrace me, fiends and wicked men,
For I am of your crew.   Draw back,
Pure women, children with clear eyes,
Let Scorn confess me on his rack,—
Stretched down by force, uplooking then
Into the solemn skies.

Singly we pass the gloomy gate;
Some robed in honour, full of peace,
Who of themselves are not aware,
Being fed with secret wickedness,
And comforted with lies: my fate
Moves fast; I shall come there..

With all so usual, hour by hour,
And feeble will so lightly twirled
By every little breeze of sense,—
Lay'st thou to heart this common world?
Lay'st thou to heart the Ruling Power,
Just, infinite, intense?

Thou wilt not frown, O God.   Yet we
Escape not thy transcendent law;
It reigns within us and without.

I

What earthly vision never saw
Man's naked soul may suddenly see,
Dreadful, past thought or doubt.

WILLIAM ALLINGHAM.

LOST DAYS.

THE lost days of my life until to-day,
    What were they, could I see them on the street
Lie as they fell?   Would they be ears of wheat
Sown once for food but trodden into clay?
Or golden coins squandered and still to pay?
    Or drops of blood dabbling the guilty feet?
    Or such spilt water as in dreams must cheat
The throats of men in Hell, who thirst alway?

I do not see them here; but after death
    God knows I know the faces I shall see,
Each one a murdered self, with low last breath.
    'I am thyself,—what hast thou done to me?'
'And I—and I—thyself,' (lo! each one saith,)
    'And thou thyself to all eternity!'

DANTE GABRIEL ROSSETTI.

PENANCE.

MORTAL! if e'er thy spirits faint,
    By grief or pain oppressed,
Seek not vain hope, or sour complaint,
    To cheer or ease thy breast;

But view thy bitterest pangs as sent
  A shadow of that doom
Which is the soul's just punishment
  In its own guilt's true home.

Be thine own judge: hate thy proud heart;
  And, while the sad drops flow,
E'en let thy will attend the smart
  And sanctify the woe.

JOHN HENRY NEWMAN.

MULTUM DILEXIT.

SHE sat and wept beside his feet; the weight
  Of sin oppressed her heart; for all the blame
And the poor malice of the worldly shame,
To her was past, extinct and out of date;
Only the sin remained,—the leprous state;
She would be melted by the heat of love,
By fires far fiercer than are blown to prove
And purge the silver ore adulterate.
She sat and wept, and with her untressed hair
Still wiped the feet she was so blest to touch;
And He wiped off the soiling of despair
From her sweet soul because she loved so much.
I am a sinner, full of doubts and fears,
Make me a humble thing of love and tears.

HARTLEY COLERIDGE.

I 2

MAY BE THE LORD WILL LOOK UPON
MY TEARS.

DROP, drop slow tears !
　　And bathe those beauteous feet,
Which brought from heaven
　　The news and Prince of Peace.
Cease not, wet eyes,
　　His mercies to entreat :
To cry for vengeance
　　Sin doth never cease.
In your deep floods
　　Drown all my faults and fears,
Nor let his eye
　　See sin but through my tears.

　　　　　　　　PHINEAS FLETCHER.

Prayer and Aspiration.

---·---

SEEKING GOD.

FAIN would my thoughts fly up to Thee,
　　Thy peace, sweet Lord, to find ;
But, when I offer, still the world
　　Lays clogs upon my mind.

Sometimes I climb a little way
　　And thence look down below ;—
How nothing, there, do all things seem,
　　That here make such a show !

Then round about I turn my eyes
　　To feast my hungry sight ;
I meet with heaven in every thing,
　　In every thing delight.

I see thy wisdom ruling all,
　　And it with joy admire ;
I see myself among such hopes
　　As set my heart on fire.

When I have thus triumphed awhile,
   And think to build my nest,
Some cross conceits come fluttering by,
   And interrupt my rest.

Then to the earth again I fall,
   And from my low dust cry,
'Twas not in my wing, Lord, but thine,
   That I got up so high.

And now, my God, whether I rise,
   Or still lie down in dust,
Both I submit to thy blest will;
   In both, on Thee I trust.

Guide Thou my way, who art Thyself
   My everlasting End,
That every step, or swift, or slow,
   Still to Thyself may tend!

                              JOHN AUSTIN.

THE SHOWER.

'TWAS so; I saw thy birth. That drowsy lake
   From   her   faint bosom   breathed   thee, the
      disease
Of her sick waters and infectious ease:
      But now at even,
      Too gross for heaven,
Thou fall'st in tears, and weep'st for thy mistake.

Ah! it is so with me. Oft have I prest
Heaven with a lazy breath ; but fruitless this
Pierced not. Love only can, with quick access,
     Unlock the way
     When all else stray—
The smoke and exhalations of the breast.

Yet if, as thou dost melt, and with thy train
Of drops make soft the earth, my eyes could weep
O'er my hard heart that's bound up and asleep,
     Perhaps at last,
     Some such showers past,
My God would give a sunshine after rain.

HENRY VAUGHAN.

DRYNESS IN PRAYER.

OH for the happy days gone by,
    When love ran smooth and free,
Days when my spirit so enjoyed
    More than earth's liberty !

Oh for the times when on my heart
    Long prayer had never palled,
Times when the ready thought of God
    Would come when it was called !

Then, when I knelt to meditate,
    Sweet thoughts came o'er my soul,
Countless and bright and beautiful,
    Beyond my own control.

What can have locked those fountains up ?
    Those visions what hath stayed ?
What sudden act hath thus transformed
    My sunshine into shade ?

This freezing heart, O Lord ! this will
    Dry as the desert sand,
Good thoughts that will not come, bad thoughts
    That come without command,

A faith that seems not faith, a hope
    That cares not for its aim,
A love that none the hotter grows
    At thy most blessed Name,

The weariness of prayer, the mist
    O'er conscience overspread,
The chill repugnance to frequent
    The feast of angel's bread :

If this drear change be thine, O Lord
    If it be thy sweet will,
Spare not, but to the very brim
    The bitter chalice fill.

But if it hath been sin of mine,
    Then show that sin to me,
Not to get back the sweetness lost
    But to make peace with Thee.

One thing alone, dear Lord ! I dread ;—
    To have a secret spot
That separates my soul from Thee,
    And yet to know it not.

For when the tide of graces set
    So full upon my heart,
I know, dear Lord ! how faithlessly
    I did my little part.

I know how well my heart hath earned
    A chastisement like this,
In trifling many a grace away
    In self-complacent bliss.

But if this weariness hath come
    A present from on high,
Teach me to find the hidden wealth
    That in its depths may lie.

So in this darkness I may learn
    To tremble and adore,
To sound my own vile nothingness,
    And thus to love Thee more,—

To love Thee, and yet not to think
    That I can love so much,—
To have Thee with me, Lord ! all day,
    Yet not to feel thy touch.

If I have served Thee, Lord! for hire,
    Hire which thy beauty showed,
Can I not serve Thee now for nought,
    And only as my God?

Thrice blessed be this darkness then,
    This deep in which I lie,
And blessed be all things that teach
    God's dear supremacy!

FREDERICK WILLIAM FABER.

PRAYER.

THERE is an awful quiet in the air,
    And the sad earth, with moist imploring eye,
Looks wide and wakeful at the pondering sky,
Like patience slow subsiding to despair.
But see, the blue smoke, as a voiceless prayer,
Sole witness of a secret sacrifice,
Unfolds its tardy wreaths, and multiplies
Its soft chameleon breathings in the rare
Capacious ether;—so it fades away,
And nought is seen beneath the pendent blue,
The undistinguishable waste of day.
So have I dreamed—oh, may the dream be true!—
That praying souls are purged from mortal hue,
And grow as pure as He to whom they pray.

HARTLEY COLERIDGE.

BE NOT AFRAID TO PRAY.

B E not afraid to pray—to pray is right.
　　Pray, if thou canst, with hope; but ever pray,
Though hope be weak, or sick with long delay:
Pray in the darkness, if there be no light.
Far is the time, remote from human sight,
When war and discord on the earth shall cease;
Yet every prayer for universal peace
Avails the blessed time to expedite.
Whate'er is good to wish, ask that of Heaven,
Though it be what thou canst not hope to see:
Pray to be perfect, though material leaven
Forbid the spirit so on earth to be:
But if for any wish thou darest not pray,
Then pray to God to cast that wish away.

　　　　　　　　　　　　HARTLEY COLERIDGE.

VENI CREATOR.

O THOU who, as our knowledge grows,
　　In the world's latter days,
The more Thou seem'st to clear the sky,
　　The more dost hide thy face:

—As ever-widening search reveals
　　The depth and breadth of ill
Scourging mankind through all the past,
　　And sweeping o'er us still:

As Science, forging day by day
Her close-linked chain, withdraws
The once-felt touches of thy hand
For dumb organic laws :

As fears of change, and fears of doubt,
Unnerve the o'er-wrought mind,
Enfeebled 'mid its added strength,
'Mid all its seeing, blind :

The wider wisdom Thou hast given
Yet is not wholly gain ;
The truer vision scathes our sight ;
We cannot see Thee plain.

Enlarge our hearts and purge our eyes
To bear thy nearer light ;
The world's young ignorance is o'er ;
Make us to know Thee right.

FRANCIS TURNER PALGRAVE.

THE ETERNITY OF GOD.

O LORD ! my heart is sick,
Sick of this everlasting change ;
And life runs tediously quick
Through its unresting race and varied range :
Change finds no likeness to itself in Thee,
And wakes no echo in thy mute eternity.

Dear Lord ! my heart is sick
Of this perpetual lapsing time,
   So slow in grief, in joy so quick,
  Yet ever casting shadows so sublime :
Time of all creatures is least like to Thee,
And yet it is our share of thine eternity.

   Oh change and time are storms
  For lives so thin and frail as ours ;
   For change the work of grace deforms
  With love that soils, and help that overpowers ;
And time is strong, and, like some chafing sea,
It seems to fret the shores of thine eternity.

   Weak, weak, for ever weak !
  We cannot hold what we possess ;
   Youth cannot find, age will not seek,—
  Oh weakness is the heart's worst weariness :
But weakest hearts can lift their thoughts to Thee ;
It makes us strong to think of thine eternity.

   Thou hadst no youth, great God !
  An unbeginning End Thou art ;
   Thy glory in itself abode,
  And still abides in its own tranquil heart :
No age can heap its outward years on Thee :
Dear God ! Thou art Thyself thine own eternity !

   Without an end or bound
   'life lies all outspread in light ;
   Our lives feel thy life all around,
  Making our weakness strong, our darkness bright ;

Yet is it neither wilderness nor sea,
But the calm gladness of a full eternity.

Oh Thou art very great
To set Thyself so far above !
But we partake of thine estate
Established in thy strength and in thy love :
That love hath made eternal room for me
In the sweet vastness of its own eternity.

Oh Thou art very meek
To overshade thy creatures thus !
Thy grandeur is the shade we seek ;
To be eternal is thy use to us :
Ah Blessed God ! what joy it is to me
To lose all thought of self in thine eternity.

Selfwearied, Lord ! I come ;
For I have lived my life too fast :
Now that years bring me nearer home
Grace must be slowly used to make it last ;
When my heart beats too quick I think of Thee,
And of the leisure of thy long eternity.

Farewell, vain joys of earth !
Farewell, all love that is not his !
Dear God ! be Thou my only mirth,
Thy majesty my single timid bliss !
Oh in the bosom of eternity
Thou dost not weary of Thyself, nor we of Thee !
                    FREDERICK WILLIAM FABER.

STRENGTH IN PRAYER.

L ORD, what a change within us one short hour
Spent in thy presence will prevail to make,
What heavy burdens from our bosoms take,
What parchèd grounds refresh, as with a shower !
We kneel, and all around us seems to lower ;
We rise, and all, the distant and the near,
Stands forth in sunny outline, brave and clear ;
We kneel how weak, we rise how full of power.
Why, therefore, should we do ourselves this wrong,
Or others—that we are not always strong,
That we are ever overborne with care,
That we should ever weak or heartless be,
Anxious or troubled, when with us is prayer,
And joy and strength and courage are with Thee ?

RICHARD CHENEVIX TRENCH.

READINESS FOR PRAYER.

I F we with earnest effort could succeed
To make our life one long connected prayer,
As lives of some perhaps have been and are,
If, never leaving Thee, we had no need
Our wandering spirits back again to lead
Into thy presence, but continued there,
Like angels standing on the highest stair
Of the sapphire throne, this were to pray indeed.

But if distractions manifold prevail,
And if in this we must confess we fail,
Grant us to keep at least a prompt desire,
Continual readiness for prayer and praise,
An altar heaped and waiting to take fire
With the least spark, and leap into a blaze.

                    RICHARD CHENEVIX TRENCH.

AN APPEAL.

WHAT mean these slow returns of love, these
        days
Of withered prayer, of dead, unflowering praise?
These hands of twilight laid on me, to keep
Dusk veils on holy vision?   This most deep,
Most eyelid-heavy, lamentable sleep?

Lo, time is precious as it was before;
As sinful sin; my goal as unattained:
And yet I drowse, and dream, and am not pained
At God far off as ever heretofore,
At sin as flagrant as of old, or more.

Dear Lord, what can I do?   I come to Thee;
I have none other helper.   Thou art free
To save me, or to kill.   But I appeal
To thy dear love, which cannot elsewise deal
Than prove Thyself my friend, thy will my weal.

Wake, wake me, Lord!   Arouse me.   Let thy fire
Loosen these icicles, and make them drop

And run into warm tears ; for I aspire
To hold Thee faster, dearer, warmer, nigher,
And love and serve Thee henceforth without stop.

HENRY SEPTIMUS SUTTON.

QUI LABORAT ORAT.

O ONLY Source of all our light and life,
 Whom as our truth, our strength, we see and feel,
But whom the hours of mortal moral strife
 Alone aright reveal !

Mine inmost soul, before Thee inly brought,
 Thy presence owns ineffable, divine;
Chastised each rebel self-encentred thought,
 My will adoreth thine.

With eye down-dropt, if then this earthly mind
 Speechless remain, or speechless e'en depart ;
Nor seek to see—for what of earthly kind
 Can see Thee as Thou art ?—

If well assured 'tis but profanely bold
 In thought's abstractest forms to seem to see,
It dare not dare the dread communion hold
 In ways unworthy Thee ;

Oh, not unowned, Thou shalt unnamed forgive ;
 In worldly walks the prayerless heart prepare ;
And, if in work its life it seem to live,
 Shalt make that work be prayer.

K

Nor times shall lack, when, while the work it plies,
    Unsummoned powers the blinding film shall part,
And, scarce by happy tears made dim, the eyes
    In recognition start.

But, as Thou willest, give or e'en forbear
    The beatific supersensual sight,
So, with thy blessing blest, that humbler prayer
    Approach Thee morn and night.

ARTHUR HUGH CLOUGH.

TO THE SUPREME BEING.

THE prayers I make will then be sweet indeed
    If Thou the spirit give by which I pray:
My unassisted heart is barren clay,
That of its native self can nothing feed:
Of good and pious works Thou art the seed,
That quickens only where Thou say'st it may:
Unless Thou show to us thine own true way
No man can find it: Father! Thou must lead.
Do Thou, then, breathe those thoughts into my mind
By which such virtue may in me be bred
That in thy holy footsteps I may tread:
The fetters of my tongue do Thou unbind,
That I may have the power to sing of Thee,
And sound thy praises everlastingly.

WORDSWORTH (*from* MICHAEL ANGELO).

Praise and Adoration.

CHEERFULNESS.

L ORD, with what courage and delight
        I do each thing,
When thy least breath sustains my wing !
        I shine and move
        Like those above ;
        And, with much gladness,
        Quitting sadness,
Make me fair days of every night.

Affliction thus mere pleasure is ;
        And, hap what will,
If Thou be in't 'tis welcome still.
        But since thy rays
        In sunny days
        Thou dost thus lend
        And freely spend,
Ah ! what shall I return for this ?

K 2

O that I were all soul! that Thou
    Wouldst make each part
Of this poor sinful frame pure heart!
    Then would I drown
    My single one;
    And to thy praise
    A concert raise
Of Hallelujahs here below.

HENRY VAUGHAN.

A THANKSGIVING.

'Thou in faithfulness hast afflicted me.'

L ORD, in this dust thy sovereign voice
    First quickened love divine;
I am all thine,—thy care and choice:
    My very praise is thine.

I praise Thee, while thy providence
    In childhood frail I trace,
For blessings given, ere dawning sense
    Could seek or scan thy grace;

Blessings in boyhood's marvelling hour;
    Bright dreams, and fancyings strange;
Blessings, when reason's awful power
    Gave thought a bolder range;

Blessings of friends, which to my door
 Unasked, unhoped, have come;
And, choicer still, a countless store
 Of eager smiles at home.

Yet, Lord, in memory's fondest place
 I shrine those seasons sad,
When, looking up, I saw thy face
 In kind austereness clad.

I would not miss one sigh or tear,
 Heart-pang, or throbbing brow;
Sweet was the chastisement severe,
 And sweet its memory now.

Yes! let the fragrant scars abide,
 Love-tokens in thy stead,
Faint shadows of the spear-pierced side,
 And thorn-encompassed head.

And such thy tender force be still,
 When self would swerve or stray;
Shaping to Truth the froward will
 Along thy narrow way.

Deny me wealth; far, far remove
 The lure of power or name;
Hope thrives in straits, in weakness Love,
 And Faith in this world's shame.

John Henry Newman.

LIFE OF LIFE.

WHAT'S that, which, ere I spake, was gone !
　　So joyful and intense a spark
That, whilst o'erhead the wonder shone,
　　The day, before but dull, grew dark?

I do not know; but this I know,
　　That, had the splendour lived a year,
The truth that I some heavenly show
　　Did see, could not be now more clear.

This know I too : might mortal breath
　　Express the passion then inspired,
Evil would die a natural death,
　　And nothing transient be desired ;

And error from the soul would pass,
　　And leave the senses pure and strong
As sunbeams.　But the best, alas !
　　Has neither memory nor tongue.

COVENTRY PATMORE.

EASTER-DAY.

I GOT me flowers to strew thy way ;
　　I got me boughs off many a tree :
But Thou wast up by break of day,
　　And brought'st thy sweets along with Thee.

The sun arising in the East,
  Though he give light and th' East perfume;
If they should offer to contest
  With thy arising, they presume.

Can there be any day but this,
  Though many suns to shine endeavour?
We count three hundred, but we miss:
  There is but one, and that one ever.

GEORGE HERBERT.

AFTER ATTENDING A PRESBYTERIAN SERVICE.

O GOD! I thank Thee for a homely taste
  And appetite of soul, that wheresoe'er
I find thy Gospel—preachèd Word or Prayer—
Before me set, by whomsoever placed,
I love the food, and let no morsel waste:
Who serves me, who feeds with me, I less care;
All who speak truth to me commissioned are;
All who love God are in my Church embraced.
Not that I have no sense of preference—
None deeper!—but I rather love to draw,
Even here, on earth, on toward the future law,
And Heaven's fine etiquette, where Who? and
  Whence?
May not be asked; and, at the Wedding Feast,
North shall sit down with South, and West with East.

THOMAS BURBIDGE.

RODS AND KISSES.

ALL blessings ask a blessed mood;
The garnish here is more than meat;
Happy who takes sweet gratitude;
Next best, though bitter, is regret.

'Tis well if, on the tempest's gloom,
You see the covenant of God;
But far, far happier he on whom
The kiss works better than the rod.

COVENTRY PATMORE.

GOD'S WAY.

'For my thoughts are not your thoughts, saith the Lord.'

I SAID, 'The darkness shall content my soul;'
God said, 'Let there be light.'
I said, 'The night shall see me reach my goal;'
Instead came dawning bright.

I bared my head to meet the smiter's stroke;
There came sweet dropping oil.
I waited, trembling, but the voice that spoke
Said gently, 'Cease thy toil.'

I looked for evil, stern of face and pale;
Came good, too fair to tell.
I leant on God when other joys did fail;
He gave me these as well.

SARAH WILLIAMS.

MUSIC.

THAT music breathes all through my spirit
  As the breezes blow through a tree ;
And my soul gives light as it quivers,
  Like moons on a tremulous sea.

New passions are wakened within me,
  New passions that have not a name ;
Dim truths that I knew but as phantoms
  Stand up clear and bright in the flame.

And my soul is possessed with yearnings
  Which make my life broaden and swell ;
And I hear strange things that are soundless,
  And I see the invisible.

Oh silence that clarion in mercy !
  For it carries my soul away ;
And it whirls my thoughts out beyond me,
  Like the leaves on an autumn day.

O exquisite tyranny ! silence,—
  My soul slips from under my hand,
And as if by instinct is fleeing
  To a dread unvisited land.

Is it sound, or fragrance, or vision ?
  Vocal light wavering down from above ?
Past prayer and past praise I am floating
  Down the rapids of speechless love.

I strove, but the sweet sounds have conquered :
    Within me the Past is awake ;
The Present is grandly transfigured ;
    The Future is clear as daybreak.

Now Past, Present, Future have mingled
    A new sort of Present to make ;
And my life is all disembodied,
    Without time, without space, without break.

But my soul seems floating for ever
    In an orb of ravishing sounds,
Through faint-falling echoes of heavens
    'Mid beautiful earths without bounds.

Now sighing, as zephyrs in summer,
    The concords glide in like a stream,
With a sound that is almost a silence,
    Or the soundless sounds in a dream.

Then oft, when the music is faintest,
    My soul has a storm in its bowers,
Like the thunder among the mountains,
    Like the wind in the abbey towers.

There are sounds, like flakes of snow falling
    In their silent and eddying rings ;
We tremble,—they touch us so lightly,
    Like the feathers from angels' wings.

There are pauses of marvellous silence,
   That are full of significant sound,
Like music echoing music
   Under water or under ground.

That clarion again ! through what valleys
   Of deep inward life did it roll,
Ere it blew that astonishing trumpet
   Right down in the caves of my soul ?

My mind is bewildered with echoes,—
   Not all from the sweet sounds without;
But spirits are answering spirits
   In a beautiful muffled shout.

Oh cease then, wild horns ! I am fainting ;
   If ye wail so, my heart will break ;
Some one speaks to me in your speaking
   In a language I cannot speak.

Though the sounds ye make are all foreign,
   How native, how household they are ;
The tones of old homes mixed with heaven,
   The dead and the angels, speak there.

Dear voices, that long have been silenced,
   Come clear from their peaceable land,
Come toned with unspeakable sweetness
   From the Presence in which they stand.

Or is music the inarticulate
  Speech of the angels on earth?
Or the voice of the Undiscovered
  Bringing great truths to the birth?

O music! thou surely art worship;
  But thou art not like praise or prayer;
And words make better thanksgiving
  Than thy sweet melodies are.

There is in thee another worship,
  An outflow of something divine;
For the voice of adoring silence,
  If it could be a voice, were thine.

Thou art fugitive splendours made vocal,
  As they glanced from that shining sea
Where the Vision is visible music,
  Making music of spirits who see.

Thou, Lord, art the Father of music;
  Sweet sounds are a whisper from Thee;
Thou hast made thy creation all anthems,
  Though it singeth them silently.

But I guess by the stir of this music
  What raptures in heaven can be,
Where the sound is thy marvellous stillness,
  And the music is light out of Thee.

FREDERICK WILLIAM FABER.

MY PSALM.

I MOURN no more my vanished years :
  Beneath a tender rain,
An April rain of smiles and tears,
  My heart is young again.

The west-winds blow, and, singing low,
  I hear the glad streams run ;
The windows of my soul I throw
  Wide open to the sun.

No longer forward, nor behind,
  I look in hope or fear;
But, grateful, take the good I find,
  The best of now and here.

I plough no more a desert land,
  To harvest weed and tare ;
The manna dropping from God's hand
  Rebukes my painful care.

I break my pilgrim staff, I lay
  Aside the toiling oar ;
The angel sought so far away
  I welcome at my door.

The airs of spring may never play
  Among the ripening corn,
Nor freshness of the flowers of May
  Blow through the autumn morn ;

Yet shall the blue-eyed gentian look
  Through fringèd lids to heaven ;
And the pale aster in the brook
  Shall see its image given ;

The woods shall wear their robes of praise,
  The south-wind softly sigh,
And sweet, calm days in golden haze
  Melt down the amber sky.

Not less shall manly deed and word
  Rebuke an age of wrong :
The graven flowers that wreathe the sword
  Make not the blade less strong.

But smiting hands shall learn to heal,—
  To build, as to destroy ;
Nor less my heart for others feel
  That I the more enjoy.

All as God wills, who wisely heeds
  To give or to withhold,
And knoweth more of all my needs
  Than all my prayers have told.

Enough that blessings undeserved
  Have marked my erring track ;
That wheresoe'er my feet have swerved
  His chastening turned me back ;

That more and more a Providence
    Of love is understood,
Making the springs of time and sense
    Sweet with eternal good ;

That death seems but a covered way
    Which opens into light,
Wherein no blinded child can stray
    Beyond the Father's sight ;

That care and trial seem at last,
    Through memory's sunset air,
Like mountain-ranges overpast,
    In purple distance fair ;

That all the jarring notes of life
    Seem blending in a psalm,
And all the angles of its strife
    Slow rounding into calm.

And so the shadows fall apart
    And so the west-winds play ;
And all the windows of my heart
    I open to the day.

            JOHN GREENLEAF WHITTIER.

Faith.

STRONG SON OF GOD.

STRONG Son of God, immortal Love,
  Whom we, that have not seen thy face,
  By faith, and faith alone, embrace,
Believing where we cannot prove ;

Thine are these orbs of light and shade ;
  Thou madest Life in man and brute ;
  Thou madest Death ; and lo, thy foot
Is on the skull which Thou hast made.

Thou wilt not leave us in the dust :
  Thou madest man, he knows not why ;
  He thinks he was not made to die ;
And Thou hast made him : Thou art just.

Thou seemest human and divine,
  The highest, holiest manhood Thou :
  Our wills are ours, we know not how ;
Our wills are ours to make them thine.

Our little systems have their day ;
  They have their day and cease to be :
  They are but broken lights of Thee,
And Thou, O Lord, art more than they.

We have but faith : we cannot know ;
  For knowledge is of things we see ;
  And yet we trust it comes from Thee,
A beam in darkness : let it grow.

Let knowledge grow from more to more,
  But more of reverence in us dwell ;
  That mind and soul, according well,
May make one music as before,

But vaster.   We are fools and slight ;
  We mock Thee when we do not fear ;
  But help thy foolish ones to bear ;
Help thy vain worlds to bear thy light.

ALFRED TENNYSON

WITH WHOM IS NO VARIABLENESS.

IT fortifies my soul to know
    That, though I perish, Truth is so ;
That, howsoe'er I stray and range,
Whate'er I do, Thou dost not change.
I steadier step when I recall
That, if I slip, Thou dost not fall.

ARTHUR HUGH CLOUGH.

CALL ON US.

WHEN the enemy is near thee,
          Call on us !
In our hands we will upbear thee,
He shall neither scathe nor scare thee,
He shall fly thee and shall fear thee.
          Call on us !

Call when all good friends have left thee,
Of all good sights and sounds bereft thee ;
Call when hope and heart are sinking,
When the brain is sick with thinking,—
          Help, O, help !
Call, and following close behind thee,
There shall haste and there shall find thee,
          Help, sure help.

When the panic comes upon thee,
When necessity seems on thee,
Hope and choice have all foregone thee,
Fate and force are closing o'er thee,
And but one way stands before thee,
          Call on us !

Oh, and if thou dost not call,
Be but faithful, that is all.
Go right on, and close behind thee,
There shall follow still and find thee,
          Help, sure help.
                    ARTHUR HUGH CLOUGH.

EVIDENCES OF RELIGION.

YE who would build the Churches of the Lord,
　　See that ye make the western portals low :
Let no one enter who disdains to bow.
High truths profanely gazed at, unadored,
Will be abused at first, at last abhorred ;
And many a learned, many a lofty brow
Hath rested, pillowed on a humbler vow
Than keen logicians notice or record.
O stainless peace of blest Humility !
Of all who fain would enter, few, alas !
Catch the true meaning of that kind, sad eye ;
While thou, God's portress, stationed by the door,
Dost stretch thy cross so near the marble floor,
That children only without bending pass.

AUBREY DE VERE.

A CHILD'S THOUGHT OF GOD.

THEY say that God lives very high ;
　　But if you look above the pines
You cannot see our God ; and why ?

And if you dig down in the mines
　　You never see Him in the gold ;
Though from Him all that's glory shines.

L 2

God is so good, He wears a fold
  Of heaven and earth across his face—
Like secrets kept, for love, untold

But still I feel that his embrace
  Slides down by thrills, through all things made,
Through sight and sound of every place.

As if my tender mother laid
  On my shut lips her kisses' pressure,
Half-waking me at night, and said,
  ' Who kissed you through the dark, dear guesser ?'

                ELIZABETH BARRETT BROWNING.

THE WILL OF GOD.

I WORSHIP thee, sweet Will of God,
    And all thy ways adore ;
And every day I live I seem
    To love thee more and more.

Thou wert the end, the blessed rule
    Of our Saviour's toils and tears ;
Thou wert the passion of his heart
    Those three-and-thirty years.

And He hath breathed into my soul
    A special love of thee,
A love to lose my will in his
    And by that loss be free.

I love to kiss each print where thou
    Hast set thine unseen feet :
I cannot fear thee, blessed Will !
    Thine empire is so sweet.

When obstacles and trials seem
    Like prison walls to be,
I do the little I can do,
    And leave the rest to thee.

I have no cares, O blessed Will !
    For all my cares are thine ;
I live in triumph, Lord ! for Thou
    Hast made thy triumphs mine.

And when it seems no chance or change
    From grief can set me free,
Hope finds its strength in helplessness,
    And gaily waits on Thee.

Man's weakness waiting upon God,
    Its end can never miss,
For men on earth no work can do
    More angel-like than this.

Ride on, ride on, triumphantly,
    Thou glorious Will ! ride on ;
Faith's pilgrim sons behind thee take
    The road that thou hast gone.

He always wins who sides with God
    To him no chance is lost :
God's will is sweetest to him when
    It triumphs at his cost.

Ill that He blesses is our good,
    And unblest good is ill ;
And all is right that seems most wrong
    If it be his sweet will.

FREDERICK WILLIAM FABER.

FAITH.

'F OLLOW me,' Jesus said ; and they uprose,
    Peter and Andrew rose and followed Him,
Followed Him even to heaven through death most
    grim,
And through a long hard life without repose,
Save in the grand ideal of its close.
    'Take up your cross and come with me,' He said ;
    And the world listens yet through all her dead,
And still would answer had we faith like those.

But who can light again such beacon-fire !
    With gladsome haste and with rejoicing souls—
    How would men gird themselves for the emprise ?
Leaving their black boats by the dead lake's mire,
    Leaving their slimy nets by the cold shoals,
    Leaving their old oars, nor once turn their eyes.

WILLIAM BELL SCOTT.

O GOD, IMPART THY BLESSING.

O GOD, impart thy blessing to my cries !
 I trust but faintly, and I daily err ;
The waters of my heart are oft astir,
An angel's there ! and yet I cannot rise.
Ah ! would my Lord were here amongst us still,
 Proffering his bosom to his servant's brow !
 Too oft that holy life comes o'er us now
Like twilight echoes from a distant hill :
We long for his pure looks and words sublime ;
 His lowly-lofty innocence and grace ;
His talk sweet-toned, and blessing all the time ;
 The mountain sermon and the ruthful gaze ;
 The cheerly credence gathered from his face ;
His voice in village groups at eve or prime.

CHARLES TURNER.

FAITH AND SIGHT IN THE LATTER DAYS.

'I præ : sequar.'

THOU say'st, 'Take up thy cross,
 O Man, and follow me :'
The night is black, the feet are slack,
 Yet we would follow Thee.

But O, dear Lord, we cry,
 That we thy face could see !

Thy blessed face one moment's space—
    Then might we follow Thee !

Dim tracts of time divide
    Those golden days from me ;
Thy voice comes strange o'er years of change ;
    How can I follow Thee ?

Comes faint and far thy voice
    From vales of Galilee ;
Thy vision fades in ancient shades ;
    How should we follow Thee ?

Unchanging law binds all,
    And Nature all we see :
Thou art a star, far off, too far,
    Too far to follow Thee !

—Ah, sense-bound heart and blind !
    Is nought but what we see?
Can time undo what once was true ;
    Can we not follow Thee ?

Is what we trace of law
    The whole of God's decree ?
Does our brief span grasp Nature's plan,
    And bid not follow Thee ?

O heavy cross—of faith
    In what we cannot see !
As once of yore, thyself restore
    And help to follow Thee !

If not as once Thou cam'st
  In true humanity,
Come yet as guest within the breast
  That burns to follow Thee.

Within our heart of hearts
  In nearest nearness be :
Set up thy throne within thine own :—
  · Go, Lord : we follow Thee.

FRANCIS TURNER PALGRAVE.

LOW SPIRITS.

FEVER, and fret, and aimless stir,
    And disappointed strife,
All chafing unsuccessful things,
    Make up the sum of life.

Love adds anxiety to toil,
    And sameness doubles cares,
· While one unbroken chain of work
    The flagging temper wears.

The light and air are dulled with smoke ;
    The streets resound with noise ;
And the soul sinks to see its peers
    Chasing their joyless joys.

Voices are round me, smiles are near,
    Kind welcomes to be had ;
And yet my spirit is alone,
    Fretful, outworn, and sad.

A weary actor, I would fain
   Be quit of my long part:
The burden of unquiet life
   Lies heavy on my heart.

Sweet thought of God ! now do thy work,
   As thou hast done before ;
Wake up, and tears will wake with thee,
   And the dull mood be o'er.

The very thinking of the thought
   Without or praise or prayer,
Gives light to know, and life to do,
   And marvellous strength to bear.

Oh, there is music in that thought
   Unto a heart unstrung,
Like sweet bells at the evening time
   Most musically rung.

'Tis not his justice or his power,
   Beauty or blest abode,
But the mere unexpanded thought
   Of the Eternal God.

It is not of his wondrous works,
   Nor even that He is ;
Words fail it, but it is a thought
   Which by itself is bliss.

Sweet thought ! lie closer to my heart,
   That I may feel thee near,

As one who for his weapon feels
   In some nocturnal fear.

Mostly in hours of gloom thou com'st,
   When sadness makes us lowly,
As though thou wert the echo sweet
   Of humble melancholy.

I bless Thee, Lord, for this kind check
   To spirits over free,
And for all things that make me feel
   More helpless need of Thee.

FREDERICK WILLIAM FABER.

SOWING IN FAITH.

NATURE'S least worthy growths have quickest
   spring,
And soonest answering service readiest meed,
And undiscerning glory's shining wing
Lights earliest on an ill-deserving head.
Winter o'er autumn-scattered wheat doth fling
A white oblivion that keeps warm the seed ;
And wisest thought needs deepest burying,
Before its ripe effect begins to breed.
Therefore, O spiritual seedsman, cast
With unregretful hand thy rich grain forth,
Nor think thy word's regenerating birth
Dead, that so long lies locked in human breast.
Time, slow to foster things of lesser worth,
Broods o'er thy work, and God permits no waste.

WILLIAM CALDWELL ROSCOE.

THE FLOWER.

H OW fresh, O Lord, how sweet and clean
        Are   thy   returns !   even   as   the   flowers   in
    spring;
To which, besides their own demean,
The late-past frosts tributes of pleasure bring.
        Grief melts away
        Like snow in May,
As if there were no such cold thing.

Who would have thought my shrivelled heart
Could have recovered greenness ?   It was gone
    Quite underground, as flowers depart
To see their mother root, when they have blown ;
        Where they together
        All the hard weather,
Dead to the world, keep house unknown.

These are thy wonders, Lord of power,
Killing and quickening, bringing down to hell
    And up to heaven in an hour ;
Making a chiming of a passing bell.
        We say amiss
        This or that is :
Thy word is all, if we could spell.

O that I once past changing were,
Fast in thy Paradise where no flower can wither !

Many a spring I shoot up fair,
Offering at heaven, growing and groaning thither;
    Nor doth my flower
    Want a spring-shower,
My sins and I joining together.

But while I grow in a straight line,
Still upwards bent as if heaven were mine own,
    Thy anger comes, and I decline:
What frost to that? what pole is not the zone
    Where all things burn,
    When Thou dost turn,
And the least frown of thine is shown.

And now in age I bud again;
After so many deaths I live and write;
    I once more smell the dew and rain,
And relish versing. O my only Light,
    It cannot be
    That I am he,
On whom thy tempests fell all night.

These are thy wonders, Lord of love!
To make us see we are but flowers that glide:
    Which when we once can find and prove,
Thou hast a garden for us, where to bide.
    Who would be more,
    Swelling through store,
Forfeit their Paradise by their pride.

GEORGE HERBERT.

THE HIDDEN FLOWER.

I WALKED the other day, to spend my hour,
    Into a field,
Where I sometimes had seen the soil to yield
    A gallant flower:
But winter now had ruffled all the bower
    And curious store
    I knew there heretofore.

Yet I, whose search loved not to peep and peer
    I' th' face of things,
Thought with myself there might be other springs
    Besides this here
Which, like cold friends, sees us but once a year;
    And so the flower
    Might have some other bower.

Then, taking up what I could nearest spy,
    I digged about
That place where I had seen him to grow out;
    And, by and by,
I saw the warm recluse alone to lie
    Where, fresh and green,
    He lived of us unseen.

Many a question intricate and rare
    Did I there strow;
But all I could extort was, that he now
    Did there repair

Such losses as befell him in this air,
    And would ere long
Come forth most fair and young.

This past, I threw the clothes quite o'er his head ;
    And, stung with fear
Of my own frailty, dropped down many a tear
    Upon his bed ;
Then sighing whispered ' Happy are the dead !
    What peace doth now
Rock him asleep below ! '

And yet how few believe such doctrine springs
    From a poor root
Which, all the winter, sleeps here under foot,
    And hath no wings
To raise it to the truth and light of things,
    But is still trod
By every wandering clod.

O Thou whose Spirit did at first inflame
    And warm the dead,
And by a sacred incubation fed
    With life this frame,
Which once had neither being, form nor name,
    Grant I may so
Thy steps track here below,

That in these masks and shadows I may see
    Thy sacred way ;
And by those hid ascents climb to that day
    Which breaks from Thee

Who art in all things though invisibly.
Show me thy peace,
Thy mercy, love and ease.

And from this care, where dreams and sorrows reign,
Lead me above,
Where light, joy, leisure and true comforts move
Without all pain.
There, hid in Thee, show me his life again
At whose dumb urn
Thus all the year I mourn.

HENRY VAUGHAN.

THE SOUL.

IS not the body more than meat? The soul
Is something greater than the food it needs:
Prayers, sacraments, and charitable deeds,
They realize the hours that onward roll
Their endless way, ' to kindle or control.'
Our acts and words are but the pregnant seeds
Of future being, when the flowers and weeds,
Local and temporal, in the vast whole
Shall live eternal. Nothing ever dies!
The shortest smile that flits across a face
Which lovely grief hath made her dwelling-place,
Lasts longer than the earth or visible skies!
It is an act of God, whose acts are truth,
And vernal still in everlasting youth.

HARTLEY COLERIDGE.

LIFE STRUGGLES.

I.

WE asked not to be born : 'tis not by will
    That we are here beneath the battle-smoke,
Without escape ; by good things as by ill,
    By facts and mysteries enchained : no cloak
Of an Elijah, no stairs whereupon
    Angels ascending and descending shine
Over the head here pillowed on a stone, ،
    Anywhere found ; so say they who repine.
But each year hath its harvest, every day
    Some clang of cymbals, laughter, or sweet moan ;
Yea, thought itself is triumph, nor would I pray
    For rest, or shrink, if I could but command
Courage of heart,— courage of heart and hand.

II.

Courage of heart and hand, Faith first of all :
    Such is the prayer of the perplexèd man,
Mistrusting the still voice, and its true call
    To work ; opposed it may be by the ban
Of social ills.   Prayer answered by desires
    Within the soul for more than sense receives,
And by sky-pointing fingers of fair spires,
    From whose kind creeds the refuged mortal weaves
Protecting garments for this pilgrim-strife,
    Passing from world to world.   But let us here,
With full breast bare to all the winds of life,
    And ready hand, and answering eye and ear,

M

Gain faith and courage through self-harmony;
Cheerful in strong repose,—fearless to live or die.

WILLIAM BELL SCOTT.

OH YET WE TRUST.

OH yet we trust that somehow good
　　Will be the final goal of ill,
　　To pangs of nature, sins of will,
Defects of doubt, and taints of blood ;

That nothing walks with aimless feet ;
　　That not one life shall be destroyed,
　　Or cast as rubbish to the void,
When God hath made the pile complete ;

That not a worm is cloven in vain ;
　　That not a moth with vain desire
　　Is shrivelled in a fruitless fire,
Or but subserves another's gain.

Behold, we know not anything ;
　　I can but trust that good shall fall
　　At last—far off—at last, to all,
And every winter change to spring.

So runs my dream : but what am I ?
　　An infant crying in the night :
　　An infant crying for the light,
And with no language but a cry.

ALFRED TENNYSON.

THY WAY IS IN THE DEEP.

THY way is in the deep, O Lord !
    E'en there we'll go with Thee:
We'll meet the tempest at thy word,
    And walk upon the sea !

Poor tremblers at his rougher wind,
    Why do we doubt Him so ?—
Who gives the storm a path, will find
    The way our feet shall go.

A moment may his hand be lost,—
    Drear moment of delay !—
We cry ' Lord ! help the tempest-tost—'
    And safe we're borne away.

The Lord yields nothing to our fears,
    And flies from selfish care ;
But comes Himself, where'er He hears
    The voice of loving prayer.

O happy soul of faith divine !
    Thy victory how sure !
The love that kindles joy is thine,—
    The patience to endure.

Come, Lord of peace ! our griefs dispel ;
    And wipe our tears away :
'Tis thine, to order all things well.
    And ours, to bless the sway.

                              ANONYMOUS.

THE PILLAR OF THE CLOUD.

L EAD, kindly Light, amid the encircling gloom,
    Lead Thou me on !
The night is dark, and I am far from home—
    Lead Thou me on !
Keep Thou my feet ; I do not ask to see
The distant scene,—one step enough for me.

I was not ever thus, nor prayed that Thou
    Shouldst lead me on.
I loved to choose and see my path ; but now
    Lead Thou me on !
I loved the garish day, and, spite of fears,
Pride ruled my will : remember not past years.

So long thy power hath blest me, sure it still
    Will lead me on,
O'er moor and fen, o'er crag and torrent, till
    The night is gone ;
And with the morn those angel faces smile
Which I have loved long since, and lost awhile.

                                JOHN HENRY NEWMAN.

Hope.

———◆———

THE WORLD'S AGE.

WHO will say the world is dying?
    Who will say our prime is past?
Sparks from Heaven, within us lying,
    Flash, and will flash till the last.
Fools ! who fancy Christ mistaken;
    Man a tool to buy and sell;
Earth a failure, God-forsaken,
    Anteroom of Hell.

Still the race of Hero-spirits
    Pass the lamp from hand to hand;
Age from age the words inherits—
    'Wife, and Child, and Fatherland.'
Still the youthful hunter gathers
    Fiery joy from wold and wood;
He will dare, as dared his fathers,
    Give him cause as good.

While a slave bewails his fetters ;
　While an orphan pleads in vain ;
While an infant lisps his letters,
　Heir of all the ages' gain ;
While a lip grows ripe for kissing ;
　While a moan from man is wrung ;
Know, by every want and blessing,
　That the world is young.

CHARLES KINGSLEY.

PUT FORTH THY LEAF.

PUT forth thy leaf, thou lofty plane,
　East winds-and frost are safely gone ;
With zephyr mild and balmy rain
　The summer comes serenely on ;
Earth, air, and sun and skies combine
　To promise all that's kind and fair :—
But thou, O human heart of mine,
　Be still, contain thyself, and bear.

December days were brief and chill,
　The winds of March were wild and drear,
And, nearing and receding still,
　Spring never would, we thought, be here.
The leaves that burst, the suns that shine,
　Had, not the less, their certain date :—
And thou, O human heart of mine,
　Be still, refrain thyself, and wait.

ARTHUR HUGH CLOUGH.

HOPE BENEATH THE WATERS.

'I CANNOT mount to heaven beneath this ban:
  Can Christian hope survive so far below
The level of the happiness of man?
Can angels' wings in these dark waters grow?'
A spirit voice replied, 'From bearing right
Our sorest burthens, comes fresh strength to bear;
And so we rise again towards the light,
And quit the sunless depths for upper air.
Meek patience is as diver's breath to all
Who sink in sorrow's sea, and many a ray
Comes gleaming downward from the source of day,
To guide us re-ascending from our fall.
The rocks have bruised thee sore, but angels' wings
Grow best from bruises, hope from anguish springs.'

CHARLES TURNER.

NOT IN VAIN.

SAY not the struggle nought availeth,
  The labour and the wounds are vain,
The enemy faints not, nor faileth,
  And as things have been they remain.

If hopes were dupes, fears may be liars;
  It may be, in yon smoke concealed,
Your comrades chase e'en now the fliers,
  And, but for you, possess the field.

For while the tired waves, vainly breaking,
    Seem here no painful inch to gain,
Far back, through creeks and inlets making,
    Comes silent, flooding in, the main.

And not by eastern windows only,
    When daylight comes, comes in the light,
In front, the sun climbs slow, how slowly,
    But westward, look, the land is bright.

ARTHUR HUGH CLOUGH.

THE PATIENCE OF HOPE.

BLASPHEME not thou thy sacred life, nor turn
    O'er joys that God hath for a season lent,
Perchance to try thy spirit and its bent,
Effeminate soul and base ! weakly to mourn.
There lies no desert in the land of life ;
For e'en that tract that barrenest doth seem,
Laboured of thee in faith and hope, shall teem
With heavenly harvests and rich gatherings rife.
Haply no more music and mirth and love,
And glorious things of old and younger art,
Shall of thy days make one perpetual feast ;
But, when these bright companions all depart,
Lay thou thy head upon the ample breast
Of Hope, and thou shalt hear the angels sing above.

FRANCES ANNE KEMBLE.

THROUGH A GLASS DARKLY.

WHAT we, when face to face we see
　　The Father of our souls, shall be,
John tells us, doth not yet appear ;
Ah, did he tell what we are here !

A mind for thoughts to pass into,
A heart for loves to travel through,
Five senses to detect things near,
Is this the whole that we are here ?

Rules baffle instincts—instincts rules,
Wise men are bad—and good are fools,
Facts evil—wishes vain appear,
We cannot go, why are we here ?

Oh may we, for assurance sake,
Some arbitrary judgment take,
And wilfully pronounce it clear,
For this or that 'tis we are here ?

Or is it right, and will it do,
To pace the sad confusion through,
And say :—' It doth not yet appear
What we shall be, what we are here '?

Ah yet, when all is thought and said,
The heart still overrules the head ;

Still what we hope we must believe,
And what is given us receive ;

Must still believe, for still we hope,
That, in a world of larger scope,
What here is faithfully begun
Will be completed, not undone.

My child, we still must think, when we
That ampler life together see,
Some true result will yet appear
Of what we are, together, here.

ARTHUR HUGH CLOUGH.

SOME FUTURE DAY.

SOME future day, when what is now is not,
    When all old faults and follies are forgot,
And thoughts of difference passed like dreams away,
We'll meet again, upon some future day.

When all that hindered, all that vexed our love,
As tall rank weeds will climb the blade above,
When all but it has yielded to decay,
We'll meet again, upon some future day.

When we have proved, each on his course alone,
The wider world, and learnt what's now unknown,
Have made life clear, and worked out each a way,
We'll meet again,—we shall have much to say.

With happier mood, and feelings born anew,
Our boyhood's bygone fancies we'll review,
Talk o'er old talks, play as we used to play,
And meet again, on many a future day.

Some day, which oft our hearts shall yearn to see,
In some far year, though distant yet to be,
Shall we indeed,—ye winds and waters say !—
Meet yet again, upon some future day ?

ARTHUR HUGH CLOUGH.

SENSE, IF YOU CAN FIND IT.

L IKE one pale, flitting, lonely gleam
      Of sunshine on a winter's day,
There came a thought upon my dream,
I know not whence, but fondly deem
      It came from far away.

Those sweet, sweet snatches of delight
      That visit our bedarkened clay,
Like passage birds, with hasty flight,—
It cannot be they perish quite,
      Although they pass away.

They come and go, and come again ;
      They're ours whatever time they stay ;
Think not, my heart, they come in vain,
If one brief while they soothe thy pain
      Before they pass away.

But whither go they ?   No one knows
    Their home,—but yet they seem to say,
That, far beyond this gulf of woes,
There is a region of repose
    For them that pass away.

                                HARTLEY COLERIDGE.

THE FUTURE.

A FIGURE wanders through my dreams
    And wears a veil upon its face,
Still bending to my breast it seems,
    Yet ever turns from my embrace.
And sometimes, passing from my sight,
    It lifts the veil as it departs,
And eyes flash out with such a light
    As never dawned on waking hearts.

There is no need of sound or speech
    Or toiling through the troubled years ;
The rapture of that smile can teach
    More than a century of tears.
And this I know, if it could move
    Out of my dreams into my days,
One service of unbroken love
    Should fill and crown my life with praise.

Love with no doubts and no demands,
    But generous as a southern June,—
Vast brotherhood of hearts and hands,
    Choir of a world in perfect tune ;

No shallow sunset-films to gild
    Far summits which we dare not climb,
But ceaseless charms of hope fulfilled,
    Making a miracle of time.

How sure, how calm, the picture seems !
    How near it comes, beheld, possessed !
It is not only in my dreams
    I feel that touch upon my breast.
It thrills me through the barren day,
    It holds me in the heart of strife,
No phantom-grasp that melts away,
    It seems—it is—the touch of life.

We look into the heart of flowers
    And wonder whence their bloom can rise;
The secret hope of human hours
    Is hidden deeper from our eyes.
In helpless tracts of wind and rain
    The work goes on without a sound;
And while you weep your weak ' In vain,'
    The flower is growing underground.

We know the lesson; but a cry,
    Bitter and vast, is in our ears;
One life of fruitless misery
    Shakes all our wisdom into tears.
Thronged by the clamorous griefs that say,
    ' Behold what *is*, forget what seems,'
I can but answer, ' Well-a-day;
    There *is* that figure in my dreams.'

              MENELLA BUTE SMEDLEY.

THE ONE HOPE.

WHEN vain desire at last and vain regret
　　Go hand in hand to death, and all is vain,
What shall assuage the unforgotten pain
And teach the unforgetful to forget?
Shall Peace be still a sunk stream long unmet,—
　　Or may the soul at once in a green plain
　　Stoop through the spray of some sweet life-fountain
And cull the dew-drenched flowering amulet?

Ah! when the wan soul in that golden air
　　Between the scriptured petals softly blown
　　Peers breathless for the gift of grace unknown,—
Ah! let none other written spell soe'er,
But only the one Hope's one name be there,—
　　Not less nor more, but even that word alone.

DANTE GABRIEL ROSSETTI.

SYMBOLS OF VICTORY.

YELLOW leaves on the ash-tree,
　　Soft glory in the air,
And the streaming radiance of sunshine
　　On the leaden clouds over there.

At a window a child's mouth smiling,
　　Overhung with tearful eyes,
At the flying rainy landscape
　　And the sudden opening skies.

Angels hanging from heaven,
  A whisper in dying ears,
And the promise of great salvation
  Shining on mortal fears.

A dying man on his pillow,
  Whose white soul, fled to his face,
Puts on her garment of joyfulness,
  And stretches to Death's embrace.

Passion, rapture, and blindness,
  Yearning, aching, and fears,
And Faith and Duty gazing
  With steadfast eyes upon tears.

I see, or the glory blinds me
  Of a soul divinely fair,
Peace after great tribulation,
  And victory hung in the air.

WILLIAM CALDWELL ROSCOE.

Love.

THE KINGDOM OF GOD.

I SAY to thee, do thou repeat
To the first man thou mayest meet
In lane, highway, or open street—

That he and we and all men move
Under a canopy of love
As broad as the blue sky above;

That doubt and trouble, fear and pain
And anguish, all are shadows vain,
That death itself shall not remain;

That weary deserts we may tread,
A dreary labyrinth may thread,
Through dark ways underground be led

Yet, if we will one Guide obey,
The dreariest path, the darkest way
Shall issue out in heavenly day;

And we, on divers shores now cast,
Shall meet, our perilous voyage past,
All in our Father's house at last.

And, ere thou leave him, say thou this,
Yet one word more—they only miss
The winning of that final bliss,

Who will not count it true, that Love,
Blessing, not cursing, rules above,
And that in it we live and move.

And one thing further make him know,
That to believe these things are so,
This firm faith never to forego,

Despite of all which seems at strife
With blessing, all with curses rife,
That this *is* blessing, this *is* life.

RICHARD CHENEVIX TRENCH.

LOVED ONCE.

I CLASSED, appraising once
   Earth's lamentable sounds, the 'well-a-day,'
The jarring 'yea' and 'nay,'
The fall of kisses on unanswering clay,
The sobbed 'farewell,' the 'welcome' mournfuller.—
But all did leaven the air
With a less bitter leaven of sure despair
   Than these words—'I loved once.'

N

And who saith, 'I loved once '?
Not angels, whose clear eyes love, love foresee,
Love through eternity !
And by To Love, do apprehend To Be.
Not God, called Love, his noble crown-name, casting .
A light too broad for blasting !
The great God, changing not from everlasting,
      Saith never, 'I loved once.'

      Oh ! never is 'loved once '
Thy word, thou Victim-Christ, misprizèd Friend !
Thy cross and curse may rend ;
But, having loved, Thou lovest to the end !
This is man's saying—man's !—too weak to move
One spherèd star above,
Man desecrates the eternal God-word, Love,
      By his 'no more' and 'once.'

      How say ye 'We loved once,'
Blasphemers !   Is your earth not cold enow,
Mourners, without that snow ?
Ah, friends ! and would ye wrong each other so ?
And could ye say of some, whose love is known,
Whose prayers have met your own,
Whose tears have fallen for you, whose smiles have
    shone
      So long, 'We loved them once '?

      Could ye, 'We loved her once,'
Say calm of me, sweet friends, when out of sight —
When hearts of better right
Stand in between me and your happy light ;

Or when, as flowers kept too long in the shade,
Ye find my colours fade,
And all that is not love in me decayed—
    Such words, 'Ye loved me once'?

    Could ye, 'We loved her once,'
Say cold of me, when further put away
In earth's sepulchral clay—
When mute the lips which deprecate to-day?
Not so: not then—least then—when life is shriven,
And death's full joy is given,
Of those who sit and love you up in heaven,
    Say not, 'We loved them once!'

    Say never, ye loved once!
God is too near above, the grave beneath,
And all our moments breathe
Too quick in mysteries of life and death,
For such a word. The eternities avenge
Affections light of range;
There comes no change to justify that change,
    Whatever comes—loved once!

    And yet that same word—'once'—
Is humanly acceptive! Kings have said,
Shaking a discrowned head,
'We ruled once;'—dotards, 'We once taught and led;'
Cripples 'once' danced i'the vines; and bards approved
Were once by scornings moved;
But love strikes one hour—Love. Those never loved
    Who dream that they loved once.

        ELIZABETH BARRETT BROWNING.

    N 2

FAITH, HOPE, AND CHARITY.

L OVE is the star by which our course we steer;
    Love for our kind its image glassed below;
And, when the breeze of hope begins to blow,
The radiance spreads of that dilated sphere
O'er Life's dark waters, nearer and more near.
A silver path that star appears to throw
Toward us, and with light that plain to sow
Which shakes beneath the shock of our career.
Thus is the brightness of our heavenly home
Itself a beacon unto those that stray;
The beacon thus becomes the glittering way
To all whom hope impels her seas to roam.
What then is Hope? A Faith that dares to move.
And what is Faith? The happy rest of Love.

AUBREY DE VERE.

ENOSIS.

T HOUGHT is deeper than all speech,
    Feeling deeper than all thought;
Souls to souls can never teach
    What unto themselves was taught.

We are spirits clad in veils;
    Man by man was never seen;
All our deep communing fails
    To remove the shadowy screen.

Heart to heart was never known ;
  Mind with mind did never meet ;
We are columns, left alone,
  Of a temple once complete.

Like the stars that gem the sky,
  Far apart, though seeming near,
In our light we scattered lie ;
  All is thus but starlight here.

What is social company
  But a babbling summer stream ?
What our wise philosophy
  But the glancing of a dream ?

Only when the sun of love
  Melts the scattered stars of thought ;
Only when we live above
  What the dim-eyed world hath taught ;

Only when our souls are fed
  By the Fount which gave them birth,
And by inspiration led
  Which they never drew from earth ;

We, like parted drops of rain,
  Swelling till they melt and run,
Shall be all absorbed again,
  Melting, flowing into one.

CHRISTOPHER P. CRANCH.

LOVE'S DEEP LIFE.

OUR love is not a fading, earthly flower :
   Its wingèd seed dropped down from Paradise
And, nursed by day and night, by sun and shower,
Doth momently to fresher beauty rise.
To us the leafless autumn is not bare,
Nor winter's rattling boughs lack lusty green :
Our summer hearts make summer's fulness, where
No leaf, or bud, or blossom may be seen.
For nature's life in love's deep life doth lie—
Love, whose forgetfulness is beauty's death,
Whose mystic key these cells of Thou and I
Into the infinite freedom openeth,
And makes the body's dark and narrow grate
The wide-flung leaves of Heaven's palace-gate.

                                   JAMES RUSSELL LOWELL.

LOVE IN TEARS.

IF fate Love's dear ambition mar,
   And load his breast with hopeless pain,
And seem to blot out sun and star,—
   Love, lost or won, is countless gain.
His sorrow boasts a secret bliss
   Which sorrow of itself beguiles,
And love in tears too noble is
   For pity, save of love in smiles.

But, looking backward through his tears,
    With vision of maturer scope,
How often one dead joy appears
    The platform of some better hope !
And, let us own, the sharpest smart
    Which human patience may endure
Pays light for that which leaves the heart
    More generous, dignified and pure.

COVENTRY PATMORE.

AN ANGEL IN THE HOUSE.

HOW sweet it were if, without feeble fright,
    Or dying of the dreadful beauteous sight,
An angel came to us, and we could bear
To see him issue from the silent air
At evening in our room, and bend on ours
His divine eyes, and bring us from his bowers
News of dear friends, and children, who have never
Been dead indeed,—as we shall know for ever:
Alas ! we think not what we daily see
About our hearths,—angels that are to be,
Or may be if they will, and we prepare
Their souls and ours to meet in happy air,—
A child, a friend, a wife whose soft heart sings
In unison with ours, breeding its future wings.

LEIGH HUNT.

SONNET.

L OVE in thy heart like living waters rose,
    Thine own self lost in the abounding flood;
So that with thee joy, comfort, thy life's good,
Thy youth's delights, thy beauty's freshest rose,
Were trash thy unregretful bounty chose
Before loved feet for softness to be strewed.
Such were.thy mortal temperings. Above those
Perfect, unstained, celestial, the clear brood
Of thy divine affections rose; white congress,
With brows devout, and upward-winging eyes,
At whose graced feet sacred Humility lies;
Truthfulness, Patience, Wisdom, Gentleness,
Faith, Hope, and Charity, the golden three,
And Love which casts out fear,—this was the sum of
    thee.

WILLIAM CALDWELL ROSCOE.

TO MY MOTHER.

A S Winter, in some mild autumnal days,
    Breathes such an air as youngest Spring discloses,
So age in thee renews an infant's grace,
And clothes thy cheek in soft November roses.
Time hath made friends with Beauty in thy face,
And, since the wheeling Fates must be obeyed,
White rime upon thy gracious head he lays,
But whispers gently not to be afraid;

And tenderly, like one that leads the blind,
He soothes thy lingering footsteps to the gate,
While that great Angel, who there keeps his state,
Smiles to behold with what slow feet he moves.
Move slower, gentlier yet, O Time ! or find
A way to fix her here, bound by our filial loves.

WILLIAM CALDWELL ROSCOE.

LOVE ON EARTH.

WHAT wonder man should fail to stay
    A nursling wafted from above,
The growth celestial come astray,
    That tender growth whose name is Love.

It is as if high winds in heaven
    Had shaken the celestial trees,
And to this earth below had given ·
    Some feathered seeds from one of these.

O perfect love that 'dureth long !
    Dear growth that, shaded by the palms,
And breathed on by the angels' song,
    Blooms on in heaven's eternal calms !

How great the task to guard thee here,
    Where wind is rough and frost is keen,
And all the ground with doubt and fear
    Is chequered, birth and death between !

Space is against thee—it can part ;
　　Time is against thee—it can chill ;
Words—they but render half the heart ;
　　Deeds—they are poor to our rich will.

JEAN INGELOW.

TO A FRIEND.

WHEN we were idlers with the loitering rills,
　　The need of human love we little noted ;
Our love was Nature ; and the peace that floated
On the white mist, and dwelt upon the hills,
To sweet accord subdued our wayward wills.
One soul was ours, one mind, one heart devoted,
That, wisely doting, asked not why it doted,
And ours the unknown joy which knowing kills.
But now I find how dear thou wert to me ;
That man is more than half of Nature's treasure,—
Of that fair beauty which no eye can see,
Of that sweet music which no ear can measure :
And now the streams may sing for others' pleasure,
The hills sleep on in their eternity.

HARTLEY COLERIDGE.

THE REVELATION.

AN idle poet, here and there,
　　Looks round him, but, for all the rest,
The world, unfathomably fair,
　　Is duller than a witling's jest.

Love wakes men, once a lifetime each;
   They lift their heavy lids and look;
And, lo, what one sweet page can teach
   They read with joy, then shut the book.

And some give thanks, and some blaspheme,
   And most forget: but, either way,
That, and the Child's unheeded dream,
   Is all the light of all their day.

COVENTRY PATMORE.

WHAT WERE I, LOVE.

WHAT were I, Love, if I were stripped of thee,
   If thine eyes shut me out whereby I live,—
Thou who unto my calmer soul dost give
Knowledge, and truth, and holy mystery,
Wherein truth mainly lies for those who see
Beyond the earthly and the fugitive,
Who in the grandeur of the soul believe,
And only in the Infinite are free?
Without thee I were naked, bleak, and bare
As yon dead cedar on the sea-cliff's brow;
And Nature's teachings, which come to me now
Common and beautiful as light and air,
Would be as fruitless as a stream which still
Slips through the wheel of some old ruined mill.

JAMES RUSSELL LOWELL.

ETERNAL LOVE.

L EAVE me, O love which reachest but to dust,
    And thou, my mind, aspire to higher things;
Grow rich in that which never taketh rust;
    Whatever fades but fading pleasure brings.
Draw in thy beams, and humble all thy might
    To that sweet yoke where lasting freedoms be,
Which breaks the clouds and opens forth the light
    That doth both shine and give us sight to see.
Oh, take fast hold! let that light be thy guide
    In this small course which birth draws out to death;
And think how evil becometh him to slide,
    Who seeketh heaven and comes of heavenly breath.
Then, farewell, world, thy uttermost I see:
Eternal Love, maintain thy love in me!

SIR PHILIP SIDNEY

Peace.

———◆———

THE PEACE OF GOD.

WE ask for Peace, O Lord !
　　Thy children ask thy Peace ;
Not what the world calls rest,
　　That toil and care should cease,
That through bright sunny hours
　　Calm life should fleet away,
And tranquil night should fade
　　In smiling day ;—
It is not for such Peace that we would pray.

We ask for Peace, O Lord !
　　Yet not to stand secure,
Girt round with iron pride,
　　Contented to endure,
Crushing the gentle strings
　　That human hearts should know,
Untouched by others' joy
　　Or others' woe ;—
Thou, O dear Lord, wilt never teach us so.

We ask thy Peace, O Lord!
　　Through storm, and fear, and strife,
To light and guide us on,
　　Through a long struggling life,
While no success or gain
　　Shall cheer the desperate fight,
Or nerve what the world calls
　　Our wasted might :—
Yet pressing through the darkness to the light.

It is thine own, O Lord,
　　Who toil while others sleep;
Who sow with loving care
　　What other hands shall reap:
They lean on Thee entranced
　　In calm and perfect rest;
Give us that Peace, O Lord,
　　Divine and blest,
Thou keepest for those hearts who love Thee best.

ADELAIDE ANNE PROCTER.

THE SLEEP.

'He giveth His beloved sleep.'

OF all the thoughts of God that are
　　Borne inward into souls afar,
Along the Psalmist's music deep,
Now tell me if that any is,
For gift or grace, surpassing this,
　　'He giveth His belovèd, sleep'?

What would we give to our beloved?
The hero's heart to be unmoved,
  The poet's star-tuned harp to sweep,
The patriot's voice to teach and rouse,
The monarch's crown to light the brows?—
  He giveth His belovèd, sleep.

What do we give to our beloved?
A little faith all undisproved,
  A little dust to overweep,
And bitter memories to make
The whole earth blasted for our sake;—
  He giveth His belovèd, sleep.

'Sleep soft, beloved!' we sometimes say,
Who have no tune to charm away
  Sad dreams that through the eyelids creep:
But never doleful dream again
Shall break the happy slumber when
  He giveth His belovèd, sleep.

O earth, so full of dreary noises!
O men, with wailing in your voices!
  O delvèd gold, the wailer's heap!
O strife, O curse, that o'er it fall!
God strikes a silence through you all,
  And giveth His belovèd, sleep.

His dews drop mutely on the hill,
His cloud above it saileth still,
  Though on its slope men sow and reap:

More softly than the dew is shed,
Or cloud is floated overhead,
  He giveth His belovèd, sleep.

Ay, men may wonder while they scan
A living, thinking, feeling man
  Confirmed in such a rest to keep;
But angels say, and through the word
I think their happy smile is *heard*—
  ' He giveth His belovèd, sleep.'

For me, my heart that erst did go
Most like a tired child at a show,
  That sees through tears the mummers leap,
Would now its wearied vision close,
Would, childlike, on His love repose
  Who giveth His belovèd, sleep.

And friends, dear friends, when it shall be
That this low breath is gone from me,
  And round my bier ye come to weep,
Let One, most loving of you all,
Say ' Not a tear must o'er her fall !
  He giveth His belovèd, sleep.'
                    ELIZABETH BARRETT BROWNING.

THE STARRY SKIES.

THE starry skies, they rest my soul,
  Its chains of care unbind,
And with the dew of cooling thoughts
  Refresh my sultry mind.

And, like a bird amidst the boughs,
  I rest, and sing, and rest,
Among those bright, dissevered worlds,
  As safe as in a nest.

And oft I think the starry sprays
  Swing with me where I light,
While brighter branches lure me o'er
  New gulfs of purple night.

Yes, something draws me upward there
  As morning draws the lark ;
Only my spell, whate'er it is,
  Works better in the dark.

It is as if a home was there
  To which my soul was turning,
A home not seen, but nightly proved
  By a mysterious yearning.

It seems as if no actual space
  Could hold it in its bond ;
Thought climbs its highest, still it is
  Always beyond, beyond.

Earth never feels like home, though fresh
  And full its tide of mirth ;
No glorious change we can conceive
  Would make a home of earth.

But God alone can be a home;
And his sweet Vision lies
Somewhere in that soft gloom concealed,
Beyond the starry skies.

So, as if waiting for a voice,
Nightly I gaze and sigh,
While the stars look at me silently
Out of their silent sky.

—How have I erred! God is my home,
And God Himself is here;
Why have I looked so far for Him
Who is nowhere but near?

Down in earth's duskiest vales, where'er
My pilgrimage may be,
Thou, Lord! wilt be a ready home
Always at hand for me.

I spake: but God was nowhere seen;
Was his love too tired to wait?
Ah no! my own unsimple love
Hath often made me late.

How often things already won
It urges me to win,
How often makes me look outside
For that which is within!

Our souls go too much out of self
    Into ways dark and dim:
'Tis rather God who seeks for us,
    Than we who seek for Him.

Yet surely through my tears I saw
    God softly drawing near;
How came He without sight or sound
    So soon to disappear?

God was not gone: but He so longed
    His sweetness to impart,
He too was seeking for a home,
    And found it in my heart.

Twice had I erred: a distant God
    Was what I could not bear;
Sorrows and cares were at my side;
    I longed to have Him there.

But God is never so far off
    As even to be near;
He is within: our spirit is
    The home He holds most dear.

To think of Him as by our side
    Is almost as untrue
As to remove his throne beyond
    Those skies of starry blue.

So, all the while I thought myself
Homeless, forlorn, and weary,
Missing my joy, I walked the earth
Myself God's sanctuary.

FREDERICK WILLIAM FABER.

THE NIGHT.

DEAR night! this world's defeat;
    The stop to busy fools; care's check and
      curb;
The day of spirits; my soul's calm retreat
    Which none disturb!
Christ's progress and his prayer-time;
The hours to which high heaven doth chime.

    God's silent, searching flight;
When my Lord's head is filled with dew, and all
His locks are wet with the clear drops of night;
    His still, soft call;
His knocking time; the soul's dumb watch,
When spirits their fair kindred catch.

    Were all my loud, evil days
Calm and unhaunted as is thy dark tent,
Whose peace but by some angel's wing or voice
    Is seldom rent;
Then I in heaven all the long year
Would keep, and never wander here.

But living where the sun
Doth all things wake, and where all mix and tire
Themselves and others, I consent and run
    To every mire;
And by this world's ill guiding light
Err more than I can do by night.

There is in God, some say,
A deep but dazzling darkness; as men here
Say it is late and dusky, because they
    See not all clear.
Oh for that night, where I in Him
Might live invisible and dim!

HENRY VAUGHAN.

LONGING.

MY heart is full of inarticulate pain,
    And beats laborious. Cold ungenial looks
Invade my sanctuary. Men of gain,
    Wise in success, well-read in feeble books,
No nigher come, I pray: your air is drear;
'Tis winter and low skies when ye appear!

Belovèd, who love beauty and fair truth!
    Come nearer me; too near ye cannot come:
Make me an atmosphere with your sweet youth;
    Give me your souls to breathe in, a large room:
Speak not a word, for see, my spirit lies
Helpless and dumb; shine on me with your eyes.

O all wide places, far from feverous towns !
   Great shining seas ! pine forests ! mountains wild !
Rock-bosomed shores! rough heaths ! and sheep-cropt
     downs !
   Vast pallid clouds ! blue spaces undefiled !
Room ! give me room ! give loneliness and air !
Free things and plenteous in your regions fair.

White dove of David, flying overhead,
   Golden with sunlight on thy snowy wings,
Outspeeding thee my longing thoughts are fled
   To find a home afar from men and things ;
Where in his temple, earth o'erarched with sky,
God's heart to mine may speak, my heart reply.

O God of mountains, stars, and boundless spaces !
   O God of freedom and of joyous hearts !
When thy face looketh forth from all men's faces,
   There will be room enough in crowded marts :
Brood thou around me, and the noise is o'er ;
Thy universe my closet with shut door.

Heart, heart, awake ! the love that loveth all
   Maketh a deeper calm than Horeb's cave.
God in thee, can his children's folly gall ?
   Love may be hurt, but shall not love be brave ?—
Thy holy silence sinks in dews of balm ;
Thou art my solitude, my mountain-calm.

                   GEORGE MACDONALD.

M. S.

L IKE morning, or the early buds in spring,
Or voice of children laughing in dark streets,
Or that quick leap with which the spirit greets
The old revisited mountains—some such thing
She seemed in her bright home. Joy and Delight
And full-eyed Innocence with folded wing
Sat in her face; and from her happy smiling
Clear air she shook, like star-lit summer night.
What needed pain to purge a spirit so pure?
Like fire it came,—what less than fire can be
The cleansing Spirit of God? Oh, happy she,
Able with holy patience to endure !
Her joy made peace, and those bright ores of nature
Subdued to purest gold of piety.

WILLIAM CALDWELL ROSCOE.

THE GUARDIAN ANGEL.

A PICTURE AT FANO.

D EAR and great Angel, wouldst thou only leave
That child, when thou hast done with him, for me !
Let me sit all the day here, that when eve
Shall find performed thy special ministry,
And time come for departure, thou, suspending
Thy flight, mayst see another child for tending,
Another still, to quiet and retrieve.

Then I shall feel thee step one step, no more,
From where thou standest now, to where I gaze,
—And suddenly my head is covered o'er
With those wings, white above the child who prays
Now on that tomb—and I shall feel thee guarding
Me, out of all the world ; for me discarding
Yon heaven, thy home, that waits and opes its door!

I would not look up thither past thy head
Because the door opes, like that child, I know,
For I should have thy gracious face instead,
Thou bird of God ! And wilt thou bend me low
Like him, and lay, like his, my hands together,
And lift them up to pray, and gently tether
Me as thy lamb there, with thy garment's spread ?

If this was ever granted, I would rest
My head beneath thine, while thy healing hands
Close-covered both my eyes beside thy breast,
Pressing the brain, which too much thought
expands,
Back to its proper size again, and smoothing
Distortion down till every nerve had soothing,
And all lay quiet, happy and suppressed.

How soon all worldly wrong would be repaired !
I think how I should view the earth and skies
And sea, when once again my brow was bared
After thy healing, with such different eyes.
O world, as God has made it ! all is beauty :
And knowing this, is love, and love is duty.
What further may be sought for, or declared ?

Guercino drew this angel I saw teach
  (Alfred, dear friend !)—that little child to pray,
Holding the little hands up, each to each
  Pressed gently,—with his own head turned away .
Over the earth where so much lay before him
Of work to do, though heaven was opening o'er him,
  And he was left at Fano by the beach.

We were at Fano, and three times we went
  To sit and see him in his chapel there,
And drink his beauty to our soul's content,
  —My angel with me too ; and since I care
For dear Guercino's fame (to which in power
And glory comes this picture for a dower,
  Fraught with a pathos so magnificent)

And since he did not work thus earnestly
  At all times, and has else endured some wrong—
I took one thought his picture struck from me,
  And spread it out, translating it to song.
My love is here.   Where are you, dear old friend ?
How rolls the Wairoa at your world's far end ?
  This is Ancona, yonder is the sea.

                                   ROBERT BROWNING.

O HAPPY DAYS.

O HAPPY days, O months, O years,
    Which, even in this dim world of woe,
'Tis now impossible can show
The print of grief, the stain of tears !

O blessed times, which now no more
   ` Exposed to chance or change remain ;
    Which having been, no after stain
Can dim the brightness that ye wore !

Dark shadows of approaching ill
  . Fall thick upon life's forward track ;
    But on its past they stream not back :
What once was bright remains so still.

RICHARD CHENEVIX TRENCH.

COMFORT.

SPEAK low to me, my Saviour, low and sweet
   From out the hallelujahs, sweet and low,
Lest I should fear and fall, and miss Thee so
Who art not missed by any that entreat.
Speak to me as to Mary at thy feet !
And if no precious gums my hands bestow,
Let my tears drop like amber while I go
In reach of thy divinest voice complete
In humanest affection—thus, in sooth,
To lose the sense of losing. As a child,
Whose song-bird seeks the wood for evermore,
Is sung to in its stead by mother's mouth
Till, sinking on her breast, love-reconciled,
He sleeps the faster that he wept before.

ELIZABETH BARRETT BROWNING.

PER PACEM AD LUCEM.

I DO not ask, O Lord, that life may be
    A pleasant road;
I do not ask that Thou wouldst take from me
    Aught of its load.

I do not ask that flowers should always spring
    Beneath my feet:
I know too well the poison and the sting
    Of things too sweet.

For one thing only, Lord, dear Lord, I plead:
    Lead me aright,
Though strength should falter and though heart should
    bleed,
    Through Peace to Light.

I do not ask, O Lord, that Thou shouldst shed
    Full radiance here;
Give but a ray of peace, that I may tread
    Without a fear.

I do not ask my cross to understand,
    My way to see;
Better in darkness just to feel thy hand
    And follow Thee.

Joy is like restless day; but peace divine
    Like quiet night.
Lead me, O Lord, till perfect day shall shine,
    Through Peace to Light.

ADELAIDE ANNE PROCTER.

Changes, Regrets, Longings.

MUTABILITY.

FROM low to high doth dissolution climb,
  And sink from high to low, along a scale
Of awful notes, whose concord shall not fail;
A musical but melancholy chime,
Which they can hear who meddle not with crime,
Nor avarice, nor over-anxious care.
Truth fails not; but her outward forms that bear
The longest date do melt like frosty rime
That in the morning whitened hill and plain
And is no more;—drop like the tower sublime
Of yesterday, which royally did wear
His crown of weeds, but could not even sustain
Some casual shout that broke the silent air,
Or the unimaginable touch of Time.

WILLIAM WORDSWORTH.

EUTOPIA.

THERE is a garden where lilies
 And roses are side by side ;
And all day between them in silence
 The silken butterflies glide.

I may not enter the garden,
 Though I know the road thereto ;
And morn by morn to the gateway
 I see the children go.

They bring back light on their faces ;
 But they cannot bring back to me
What the lilies say to the roses,
 Or the songs of the butterflies be.

FRANCIS TURNER PALGRAVE.

YOUTH AND AGE.

VERSE, a breeze 'mid blossoms straying,
 Where hope clung feeding, like a bee—
Both were mine ! Life went a maying
 With Nature, Hope, and Poesy,
  When I was young !
When I was young ?—Ah, woful When !
Ah ! for the change 'twixt Now and Then !
This breathing house not built with hands,
This body that does me grievous wrong,

O'er aëry cliffs and glittering sands
How lightly then it flashed along!
Like those trim skiffs, unknown of yore,
On winding lakes and rivers wide,
That ask no aid of sail or oar,
That fear no spite of wind or tide!
Nought cared this body for wind or weather
When Youth and I lived in't together.

Flowers are lovely; Love is flower-like;
   Friendship is a sheltering tree:
Oh! the joys that came down shower-like,
Of Friendship, Love, and Liberty,
      Ere I was old!
Ere I was old?—Ah woful Ere,
Which tells me Youth's no longer here!
O Youth! for years so many and sweet
'Tis known that thou and I were one;
I'll think it but a fond conceit—
It cannot be, that thou art gone!
Thy vesper-bell hath not yet tolled;—
And thou wert aye a masker bold!
What strange disguise hast now put on,
To make believe that thou art gone?
I see these locks in silvery slips,
This drooping gait, this altered size;
But springtide blossoms on thy lips,
And tears take sunshine from thine eyes!
Life is but thought: so think I will
That Youth and I are house-mates still.

Dewdrops are the gems of morning,
But the tears of mournful eve !
Where no hope is, life's a warning
That only serves to make us grieve
When we are old :—
That only serves to make us grieve
With oft and tedious taking-leave,
Like some poor nigh-related guest,
That may not rudely be dismist,
Yet hath outstayed his welcome while,
And tells the jest without the smile.

SAMUEL TAYLOR COLERIDGE.

IRREPARABLENESS.

I HAVE been in the meadows all the day
And gathered there the nosegay that you see,
Singing within myself as bird or bee,
When such do field-work on a morn of May.
But, now I look upon my flowers, decay
Has met them in my hands more fatally
Because more warmly clasped—and sobs are free
To come instead of songs. What do you say,
Sweet counsellors, dear friends? that I should go
Back straightway to the fields and gather more?
Another, sooth, may do it, but not I !
My heart is very tired, my strength is low,
My hands are full of blossoms plucked before,
Held dead within them till myself shall die.

ELIZABETH BARRETT BROWNING.

THE BURIED LIFE.

L IGHT flows our war of mocking words, and yet
       Behold, with tears mine eyes are wet !
I feel a nameless sadness o'er me roll.
Yes, yes, we know that we can jest,
We know, we know that we can smile !
But there's a something in this breast
To which thy light words bring no rest,
And thy gay smiles no anodyne ;
Give me thy hand, and hush awhile,
And turn those limpid eyes on mine,
And let me read there, love, thy inmost soul.

Alas, is even love too weak
To unlock the heart, and let it speak ?
Are even lovers powerless to reveal
To one another what indeed they feel ?
I knew the mass of men concealed
Their thoughts, for fear that if revealed
They would by other men be met
With blank indifference, or with blame reproved ;
I knew they lived and moved
Tricked in disguises, alien to the rest
Of men, and alien to themselves ! and yet
The same heart beats in every human breast.

But we, my love—doth a like spell benumb
Our hearts ?—our voices ?—must we too be dumb ?

Ah, well for us, if even we,
Even for a moment, can get free
Our heart, and have our lips unchained;
For that which seals them hath been deep ordained.

Fate, which foresaw
How frivolous a baby man would be,
By what distractions he would be possessed,
How he would pour himself in every strife,
And well-nigh change his own identity;
That it might keep from his capricious play
His genuine self, and force him to obey,
Even in his own despite, his being's law,
Bade through the deep recesses of our breast
The unregarded river of our life
Pursue with indiscernible flow its way;
And that we should not see
The buried stream, and seem to be
Eddying at large in blind uncertainty,
Though driving on with it eternally.

But often, in the world's most crowded streets,
But often, in the din of strife,
There rises an unspeakable desire
After the knowledge of our buried life,
A thirst to spend our fire and restless force
In tracking out our true, original course;
A longing to inquire
Into the mystery of this heart which beats
So wild, so deep in us, to know
Whence our thoughts come and where they go.

P

And many a man in his own breast then delves,
But deep enough, alas, none ever mines !
And we have been on many thousand lines, .
And we have shown, on each, spirit and power ;
But hardly have we, for one little hour,.
Been on our own line, have we been ourselves !
Hardly had skill to utter one of all
The nameless feelings that course through our breast,
But they course on for ever unexpressed !
And long we try in vain to speak and act
Our hidden self, and what we say and do
Is eloquent, is well—but 'tis not true !
And then we will no more be racked
With inward striving, and demand
Of all the thousand nothings of the hour
Their stupefying power ;
Ah yes, and they benumb us at our call !
Yet still, from time to time, vague and forlorn,
From the soul's subterranean depth upborne
As from an infinitely distant land,
Come airs, and floating echoes, and convey
A melancholy into all our day.

Only, but this is rare !
When a belovèd hand is laid in ours,
When, jaded with the rush and glare
Of the interminable hours,
Our eyes can in another's eyes read clear,
When our world-deafened ear
Is by the tones of a loved voice caressed,—
A bolt is shot back somewhere in our breast,

And a lost pulse of feeling stirs again.
The eye sinks inward, and the heart lies plain,
And what we mean we say, and what we would we
    know !
A man becomes aware of his life's flow,
And hears its winding murmur, and he sees
The meadows where it glides, the sun, the breeze.

And there arrives a lull in the hot race
Wherein he doth for ever chase
That flying and elusive shadow, rest.
An air of coolness plays upon his face,
And an unwonted calm pervades his breast.
And then he thinks he knows
The hills where his life rose,
And the sea where it goes.

MATTHEW ARNOLD.

THE FIRE OF DRIFT-WOOD.

WE sat within the farm-house old,
    Whose windows, looking o'er the bay,
Gave to the sea-breeze, damp and cold,
    An easy entrance, night and day.

Not far away we saw the port,—
    The strange, old-fashioned, silent town,—
The light-house,—the dismantled fort,—
    The wooden houses, quaint and brown.

We sat and talked until the night,
   Descending, filled the little room ;
Our faces faded from the sight,
   Our voices only broke the gloom.

We spake of many a vanished scene,
   Of what we once had thought and said,
Of what had been, and might have been,
   And who was changed, and who was dead ;

And all that fills the hearts of friends
   When first they feel, with secret pain,
Their lives thenceforth have separate ends,
   And never can be one again ;

The first slight swerving of the heart
   That words are powerless to express,
And leave it still unsaid in part,
   Or say it in too great excess.

The very tones in which we spake
   Had something strange, I could but mark ;
The leaves of memory seemed to make
   A mournful rustling in the dark.

Oft died the words upon our lips,
   As, suddenly, from out the fire
Built of the wreck of stranded ships,
   The flames would leap and then expire.

And, as their splendour flashed and failed,
  We thought of wrecks upon the main,—
Of ships dismasted, that were hailed
  And sent no answer back again.

The windows rattling in their frames,
  The ocean roaring up the beach,
The gusty blast, the bickering flames,—
  All mingled vaguely in our speech,

Until they made themselves a part
  Of fancies floating through the brain,—
The long-lost ventures of the heart,
  That send no answers back again.

O flames that glowed! O hearts that yearned!
  They were indeed too much akin,—
The drift-wood fire without that burned,
  The thoughts that burned and glowed within.

                    HENRY WADSWORTH LONGFELLOW.

QUA CURSUM VENTUS.

AS ships, becalmed at eve, that lay
    With canvas drooping, side by side,
Two towers of sail at dawn of day
    Are scarce, long leagues apart, descried ;

When fell the night, upsprung the breeze,
   And all the darkling hours they plied,
Nor dreamt but each the self-same seas
   By each was cleaving, side by side :

E'en so—but why the tale reveal
   Of those, whom, year by year unchanged,
Brief absence joined anew to feel,
   Astounded, soul from soul estranged.

At dead of night their sails were filled
   And onward each rejoicing steered—
Ah, neither blame, for neither willed,
   Or wist, what first with dawn appeared !

To veer, how vain ! On, onward strain,
   Brave barks ! In light, in darkness too,
Through winds and tides one compass guides—
   To that, and your own selves, be true.

But O blithe breeze ! and O great seas !
   Though ne'er, that earliest parting past,
On your wide plain they join again,
   Together lead them home at last.

One port, methought, alike they sought,
   One purpose hold where'er they fare,—
O bounding breeze, O rushing seas !
   At last, at last, unite them there !

ARTHUR HUGH CLOUGH.

A SUPERSCRIPTION.

LOOK in my face; my name is Might-have-been;
    I am also called No-more, Too-late, Farewell;
  Unto thine ear I hold the dead-sea shell
Cast up thy Life's foam-fretted feet between;
Unto thine eyes the glass where that is seen
    Which had Life's form and Love's, but by my spell
    Is now a shaken shadow intolerable,
Of ultimate things unuttered the frail screen.

Mark me, how still I am! But should there dart
    One moment through thy soul the soft surprise
    Of that winged Peace which lulls the breath of sighs,—
Then shalt thou see me smile, and turn apart
Thy visage to mine ambush at thy heart
    Sleepless with cold commemorative eyes.

DANTE GABRIEL ROSSETTI.

A SONG AGAINST SINGING.

TO E. J. H.

THEY bid me sing to thee,
    Thou golden-haired and silver-voicèd
    child—
With lips by no worse sigh than sleep's defiled—
With eyes unknowing how tears dim the sight,
And feet all trembling at the new delight
    Treaders of earth to be!

Ah no ! the lark may bring
A song to thee from out the morning cloud,
The merry river from its lilies bowed,
The brisk rain from the trees, the lucky wind
That half doth make its music, half doth find—
But *I*—I may not sing.

How could I think it right,
New-comer on our earth as, Sweet, thou art,
To bring a verse from out an human heart
Made heavy with accumulated tears,
And cross with such amount of weary years
Thy day-sum of delight ?

Even if the verse were said,
Thou, who wouldst clap thy tiny hands to hear
The wind or rain, gay bird or river clear,
Wouldst, at that sound of sad humanities,
Upturn thy bright uncomprehending eyes
And bid me play instead.

Therefore no song of mine—
But prayer in place of singing : prayer that would
Commend thee to the new-creating God
Whose gift is childhood's heart without its stain
Of weakness, ignorance, and changing vain—
That gift of God be thine !

So wilt thou aye be young,
In lovelier childhood than thy shining brow
And pretty winning accents make thee now :

Yea, sweeter than this scarce articulate sound
(How sweet !) of ' Father,' ' Mother,' shall be found
The ' ABBA ' on thy tongue.

And so, as years shall chase
Each other's shadows, thou wilt less resemble
Thy fellows of the earth who toil and tremble,
Than him thou seest not, thine angel bold
Yet meek, whose ever-lifted eyes behold
The Ever-loving's face.

ELIZABETH BARRETT BROWNING.

TWO SONNETS.

THE HAPPY HEARTS OF EARTH.

WHENCE thou hast come thou knowest not,
little brook,
Nor whither thou art bound.   Yet, wild and gay,
Pleased in thyself, and pleasing all that look,
Thou wendest, all the seasons, on thy way.
The lonely glen grows gladsome with thy play ;
Thou glidest lamb-like thro' the ghostly shade ;
To think of solemn things thou wast not made,
But to sing on, for pleasure, night and day.
Such happy hearts are wandering, crystal clear,
In the great world where men and women dwell ;
Earth's mighty shows they neither love nor fear ;
They are content to be, while I rebel ;
Out of their own delight dispensing cheer,
And ever softly whispering, ' All is well !'

FATHER, FORGIVE THY CHILD.

O SING, clear brook, sing on, while in a dream
   I feel the sweetness of the years go by !
The crags and peaks are softened now, and seem
   Gently to sleep against the gentle sky ;
   Old scenes and faces glimmer up and die,
With outlines of sweet thought obscured too long ;
   Like boys that shout at play far voices cry :
O sing ! for I am weeping at the song.
I know not what I am, but only know
   I have had glimpses tongue may never speak ;
No more I balance human joy and woe,
   But think of my transgressions and am meek.
Father ! forgive the child, who fretted so,—
   His proud heart yields,—the tears are on his cheek !

ROBERT BUCHANAN.

VESTIGIA RETRORSUM.

WHITE-THROATED swans and sedges of the
    mere
Still float, still quiver, on the shining stream ;
And underneath an antique bridge I hear
Smooth waters lapping slowly, and their gleam
Frets the cold dark wherein my boat is moored :
Nor overhead the storied elms of June
Forget to murmur, nor to welcome noon
With quiet : save when some stray breeze, allured
By fragrance of the central avenue,

Creeps, cooling ever, down the elastic arch,
And, thro' branched clifts and green inwoven shelves,
Lets in fresh glimpses of the sultry blue.
   So, year by year, regardless Nature blooms;
So, year by year, for all the far-off tombs
Of those who loved them, these impassive courts
Lay their calm shadows on the grateful sward.
No change is here, nor any peace is marred
Save ours, who, pausing in life's midday march,
Miss the dear souls of all these fair resorts,
And find, instead, our own forgotten selves.

ARTHUR MUNBY.

THE PRISONER.

I COUNT the dismal time by months and years
   Since last I felt the green sward under foot,
And the great breath of all things summer-mute
Met mine upon my lips. Now earth appears
As strange to me as dreams of distant spheres,
Or thoughts of Heaven we weep at. Nature's lute
Sounds on, behind this door so closely shut,
A strange wild music to the prisoner's ears,
Dilated by the distance, till the brain
Grows dim with fancies which it feels too fine
While ever, with a visionary pain,
Past the precluded senses, sweep and shine
Streams, forests, glades, and many a golden train
Of sunlit hills transfigured to Divine.

ELIZABETH BARRETT BROWNING.

BROKEN MUSIC.

THE mother will not turn, who thinks she hears
    Her nursling's speech first grow articulate ;
  But breathless with averted eyes elate
She sits, with open lips and open ears,
That it may call her twice.   'Mid doubts and fears
    Thus oft my soul has hearkened ; till the song,
    A central moan for days, at length found tongue,
And the sweet music welled and the sweet tears.

But now, whatever while the soul is fain
    To list that wonted murmur, as it were
The speech-bound sea-shell's low importunate strain,—
    No breath of song, thy voice alone is there,
O bitterly beloved ! and all her gain
    Is but the pang of unpermitted prayer.

                  DANTE GABRIEL ROSSETTI.

ASPIRATION.

JOY for the promise of our loftier homes !
    Joy for the promise of another birth !
For oft oppressive unto pain becomes
    The riddle of the earth.

A weary weight it lay upon my youth,
Ere I could tell of what I should complain ;
My very childhood was not free, in truth,
From something of that pain.

Hours of a dim despondency were there,
Like clouds that take its colour from the rose,
Which, knowing not the darkness of the air,
But its own sadness knows.

Youth grew in strength—to bear a stronger chain ;
In knowledge grew—to know itself a slave ;
And broke its narrower shells again, again,
To feel a wider grave.

What woe into the startled spirit sank
When first it knew the inaudible recall,
When first, in the illimitable blank,
It touched the crystal wall !

Far spreads this mystery of death and sin ;
Year beyond year in gloomy tumult rolls ;
And day encircling day clasps closer in
Our solitary souls.

Oh for the time when in our seraph wings
We veil our brows before the Eternal Throne—
The day when, drinking knowledge at its springs,
We know as we are known !

THOMAS BURRIDGE.

A CRY FOR REST.

BUT to be still ! oh but to cease awhile
    The panting breath and hurrying steps of life;
The sights, the sounds, the struggle and the strife
Of hourly being; the sharp biting file
Of action, fretting on the tightened chain
Of rough existence; all that is not pain,
But utter weariness ! Oh to be free,
But for a while, from conscious entity !
To shut the banging doors and windows wide
Of restless sense, and let the soul abide
Darkly and stilly for a little space,
Gathering its strength up to pursue the race.
O Heavens ! to rest a moment, but to rest
From this quick, gasping life, were to be blest !

FRANCES ANNE KEMBLE.

FRIENDS OF MY YOUTH.

'I came to the place of my birth, and cried, "The friends of
my youth, where are they?" and an echo answered, "Where
are they?"'

I SOUGHT you, friends of youth, in sun and shade,
    By home and hearth—but no ! ye were not there;
'Where are ye gone, beloved ones, where?' I said;
    I listened, and an echo answered, 'Where?'

Then silence fell around—upon a tomb
  I sat me down dismayed at death, and wept;
Over my senses fell a cloud of gloom,
  They sank before the mystery, and I slept.

I slept—and then before mine eyes there pressed
  Faces that showed a bliss unknown before;
The loved whom I in life had once possessed,
  Came one by one, till all were there once more.

A light of nobler worlds was round their head,
  A glow of better actions made them fair;
'The dead are there,' triumphantly I said;
  Triumphantly the echo answered, 'There!'

CAROLINE CLIVE.

HOME.

'TIS far away, dear friend, 'tis far away
    Where we were born and nurtured, and grew up.
Thither to-day, as this new gate of time
Swings on its noiseless hinges slowly back,
Through the far vista of our boyish years
Look with a saddened eye, aye! once more look,
Ere through these portals we pass idly on,
To see the coming painted on the wall.

I see a grand procession of fine hopes,
  Each with his face wrapped in a sable stole,
And turned away from me their once bright eyes,
  All mutely gazing on the snowy ground.

Then one,—still farther down,—this mournful troop
They carry on a bier hung round with frost,
The light is like a dying person's eye ;
For, oh, our passèd years shall make us weep,
Nor shall our boyish years live but in dreams.

They say our home is in a better land,
That we are pilgrims here, and on this march
We shall stop never, but with soilèd feet
Track the hard pavement with our dusty prints.
But yet to journey homeward were most fair,
And, no one knowing, burst upon their sight ;—
' Thou art come !'—' Indeed is't thou from the far land?'
That joy was in their hearts.   And, as the lake's
Calm surface is at once waked into life
By one slight move, so should my sudden sight
Arouse their peaceful feelings.   So will't be
When some pure man makes of this world a home,
All home,—both on new-years and birthdays, home ;
And all the people laugh within their hearts
That this is City of God, both then and now.

WILLIAM ELLERY CHANNING.

The Journey.

───────•───────

THE FUTURE.

A WANDERER is man from his birth.
  He was born in a ship
On the breast of the river of Time ;
Brimming with wonder and joy
He spreads out his arms to the light,
Rivets his gaze on the banks of the stream.

As what he sees is, so have his thoughts been.
Whether he wakes
Where the snowy mountainous pass,
Echoing the screams of the eagles,
Hems in its gorges the bed
Of the new-born clear-flowing stream ;
Whether he first sees light
Where the river in gleaming rings
Sluggishly winds through the plain ;
Whether in sound of the swallowing sea—
As is the world on the banks
So is the mind of the man.

Q

Vainly does each as he glides
Fable and dream
Of the lands which the river of Time
Had left ere he woke on its breast,
Or shall reach when his eyes have been closed.
Only the tract where he sails
He wots of : only the thoughts
Raised by the objects he passes are his.

Who can see the green earth any more
As she was by the sources of Time?
Who imagines her fields as they lay
In the sunshine, unworn by the plough?
Who thinks as they thought,
The tribes who then roamed on her breast,
Her vigorous primitive sons?

What girl
Now reads in her bosom as clear
As Rebekah read, when she sate
At eve by the palm-shaded well?
Who guards in her breast
As deep, as pellucid a spring
Of feeling, as tranquil, as sure?

What bard,
At the height of his vision, can deem
Of God, of the world, of the soul,
With a plainness as near,
As flashing, as Moses felt,

When he lay in the night by his flock
On the starlit Arabian waste?
Can rise and obey
The beck of the Spirit like him?

This tract which the river of Time
Now flows through with us, is the plain.
Gone is the calm of its earlier shore.
Bordered by cities, and hoarse
With a thousand cries is its stream.
And we on its breast, our minds
Are confused as the cries which we hear,
Changing and shot as the sights which we see.

And we say that repose has fled
For ever the course of the river of Time.
That cities will crowd to its edge
In a blacker incessanter line;
That the din will be more on its banks
Denser the trade on its stream,
Flatter the plain where it flows,
Fiercer the sun overhead.
That never will those on its breast
See an ennobling sight,
Drink of the feeling of quiet again.

But what was before us we know not,
And we know not what shall succeed.

Haply, the river of Time,
As it grows, as the towns on its marge

Fling their wavering lights
On a wider, statelier stream—
May acquire, if not the calm
Of its early mountainous shore,
Yet a solemn peace of its own.

And the width of the waters, the hush
Of the grey expanse where he floats,
Freshening its current and spotted with foam
As it draws to the Ocean, may strike
Peace to the soul of the man on its breast;
As the pale waste widens around him—
As the banks fade dimmer away—
As the stars come out, and the night-wind
Brings up the stream
Murmurs and scents of the infinite Sea.

MATTHEW ARNOLD.

WHERE LIES THE LAND.

WHERE lies the land to which the ship would go?
　Far, far ahead, is all her seamen know.
And where the land she travels from? Away,
Far, far behind, is all that they can say.

On sunny noons, upon the deck's smooth face,
Linked arm in arm, how pleasant here to pace;
Or, o'er the stern reclining, watch below
The foaming wake far-widening as we go.

On stormy nights, when wild north-westers rave,
How proud a thing to fight with wind and wave !
The dripping sailor on the reeling mast
Exults to bear, and scorns to wish it past.

Where lies the land to which the ship would go ?
Far, far ahead, is all her seamen know.
And where the land she travels from ?   Away,
Far, far behind, is all that they can say.

ARTHUR HUGH CLOUGH.

STARLIGHT.

DARKLING, methinks, the path of life is grown,
    And solitude and sorrow close around ;
My fellow-travellers one by one are gone,
    Their home is reached, but mine must still be
        found.
The sun that set as the last bowed his head
    To cross the threshold of his resting-place,
Has left the world devoid of all that made
    Its business, pleasure, happiness, and grace.
But I have still the desert path to trace ;
    Not with the day has my day's work an end ;
And winds and shadows through the cold air chase,
    And earth looks dark where walked we, friend with
        friend.

And yet thus wildered, not without a guide,
    I wander on amid the shades of night ;

My home-fires gleam, methinks, and round them glide
  My friends at peace, far off, but still in sight ;
For through the closing gloom mine eyesight goes
  Further in heaven than when the day was bright;
· And there, as earth still dark and darker grows,
  Shines out, for every shade, a world of light.

CAROLINE CLIVE.

ON THE SEA-BEACH.

M Y life is like a stroll upon the beach, ⌐
  As near the ocean's edge as I can go ;
My tardy steps its waves sometimes o'erreach,
  Sometimes I stay to let them overflow.

My sole employment is, and scrupulous care,
  To place my gains beyond the reach of tides,
Each smoother pebble, and each shell more rare,
  Which ocean kindly to my hand confides.

I have but few companions on the shore—
  They scorn the strand who sail upon the sea—
Yet oft I think the ocean they've sailed o'er
  Is deeper known upon the strand to me.

The middle sea contains no crimson dulse,
  Its deeper waves cast up no pearls to view ;
Along the shore my hand is on its pulse,
  And I converse with many a shipwrecked crew.

HENRY D. THOREAU.

LIFE.

L IFE! I know not what thou art,
But know that thou and I must part;
And when, or how, or where we met,
I own to me's a secret yet.

Life! we've been long together
Through pleasant and through cloudy weather;
'Tis hard to part when friends are dear—
Perhaps 'twill cost a sigh, a tear;
Then steal away, give little warning,
Choose thine own time;
Say not Good Night,—but, in some brighter clime,
Bid me Good Morning!

ANNA LÆTITIA BARBAULD.

UP-HILL.

D OES the road wind up-hill all the way?
Yes, to the very end.
Will the day's journey take the whole long day?
From morn to night, my friend.

But is there for the night a resting-place?
A roof for when the slow dark hours begin.
May not the darkness hide it from my face?
You cannot miss that inn.

Shall I meet other wayfarers at night?
  Those who have gone before.
Then must I knock, or call when just in sight?
  They will not keep you standing at that door.

Shall I find comfort, travel-sore and weak?
  Of labour you shall find the sum.
Will there be beds for me and all who seek?
  Yea, beds for all who come.

CHRISTINA ROSSETTI.

AT NOONTIDE CAME A VOICE.

AT noon-tide came a voice, 'Thou must away;
    Hast thou some look to give, some word to
        say,
Or hear, of fond farewell?'—I answered 'Nay,

'My soul hath said its farewell, long ago;
How light, when summer comes, the loosened snow
Slides from the hills! Yet tell me, where I go

'Doth any wait for me?' Then, like the clear,
Full drops of summer rain that seem to cheer
The skies they fall from, soft within mine ear,

And slow, as if to render through that sweet
Delay, a blest assurance more complete,
'Yea,' only 'yea,' was whispered me, and then
A silence that was unto it 'Amen.'

'Doth any love me there?' I said, 'or mark
Within the dull cold flint the fiery spark,
One moment flashing out into the dark?

'My spirit glowed, yet burned not to a clear,
Warm, steadfast flame, to lighten or to cheer.'
The sweet voice said, 'By things which do appear

'We judge amiss.   The flower which wears its way
Through stony chinks, lives on from day to day,
Approved for living, let the rest be gay

'And sweet as summer!   Heaven within the reed
Lists for the flute-note, in the folded seed
It sees the bud, and in the Will the Deed.'

DORA GREENWELL.

PROSPICE.

FEAR death?—to feel the fog in my throat,
      The mist in my face,
When the snows begin, and the blasts denote
      I am nearing the place,
The power of the night, the press of the storm,
      The post of the foe;
Where he stands, the Arch Fear in a visible form,
      Yet the strong man must go:
For the journey is done and the summit attained,
      And the barriers fall,

Though a battle's to fight ere the guerdon be gained,
  The reward of it all.
I was ever a fighter, so—one fight more,
  The best and the last !
I would hate that death bandaged my eyes, and fore-
    bore,
  And bade me creep past.
No ! let me taste the whole of it, fare like my peers
  The heroes of old,
Bear the brunt, in a minute pay glad life's arrears
  Of pain, darkness and cold.
For sudden the worst turns the best to the brave,
  The black minute's at end,
And the elements' rage, the fiend-voices that rave,
  Shall dwindle, shall blend,
Shall change, shall become, first a peace out of pain,
  Then a light, then thy breast,
O thou soul of my soul ! I shall clasp thee again,
  And with God be the rest !

ROBERT BROWNING.

THE GOLDEN GATE.

DIM shadows gather thickly round, and up the
    misty stair they climb,
The cloudy stair that upward leads to where the
    closèd portals shine,
Round which the kneeling spirits wait the opening of
    the Golden Gate.

And some with eager longing go, still pressing for-
ward, hand in hand,
And some, with weary step and slow, look back where
their Belovèd stand—
Yet up the misty stair they climb, led onward by the
Angel Time.

As unseen hands roll back the doors, the light that
floods the very air
Is but the shadow from within of the great glory
hidden there—
And morn and eve, and soon and late, the shadows
pass within the gate.

As one by one they enter in, and the stern portals
close once more,
The halo seems to linger round those kneeling closest
to the door :
The joy that lightened from that place shines still
upon the watcher's face.

The faint low echo that we hear of far-off music
seems to fill
The silent air with love and fear, and the world's
clamours all grow still,
Until the portals close again and leave us toiling on
in pain.

Complain not that the way is long—what road is
weary that leads there ?

But let the Angel take thy hand, and lead thee up the
    misty stair,
And then with beating heart await, the opening of
    the Golden Gate.

ADELAIDE ANNE PROCTER.

THE RETREAT.

HAPPY those early days when I
    Shined in my angel-infancy!
Before I understood this place
Appointed for my second race,
Or taught my soul to fancy aught
But a white, celestial thought;
When yet I had not walked above
A mile or two from my first love,
And looking back, at that short space,
Could see a glimpse of his bright face;
When on some gilded cloud or flower
My gazing soul would dwell an hour,
And in those weaker glories spy
Some shadows of eternity;
Before I taught my tongue to wound
My conscience with a sinful sound,
Or had the black art to dispense
A several sin to every sense,
But felt, through all this fleshly dress,
Bright shoots of everlastingness.
Oh, how I long to travel back,
And tread again that ancient track!

That I might once more reach that plain,
Where first I left my glorious train ;
From whence th' enlightened spirit sees
That shady city of palm-trees !
But ah ! my soul with too much stay
Is drunk, and staggers in the way !
Some men a forward motion love,
But I by backward steps would move,
And, when this dust falls to the urn,
In that state I came, return.

HENRY VAUGHAN.

ODE.

INTIMATIONS OF IMMORTALITY FROM RECOLLECTIONS OF EARLY CHILDHOOD.

'The Child is Father of the Man ;
And I could wish my days to be
Bound each to each by natural piety.'

I.

THERE was a time when meadow, grove, and stream,
The earth, and every common sight,
To me did seem
Apparelled in celestial light,
The glory and the freshness of a dream.
It is not now as it hath been of yore ;—
Turn wheresoe'er I may,
By night or day,
The things which I have seen I now can see no more.

II.

The rainbow comes and goes,
And lovely is the rose,
The moon doth with delight
Look round her when the heavens are bare,
Waters on a starry night
Are beautiful and fair ;
The sunshine is a glorious birth ;
But yet I know, where'er I go,
That there hath passed away a glory from the earth.

III.

Now, while the birds thus sing a joyous song,
And while the young lambs bound   '
As to the tabor's sound,
To me alone there came a thought of grief :
A timely utterance gave that thought relief,
And I again am strong :
The cataracts blow their trumpets from the steep ;
No more shall grief of mine the season wrong ;
I hear the echoes through the mountains throng,
The winds come to me from the fields of sleep,
And all the earth is gay ;
Land and sea
Give themselves up to jollity,
And with the heart of May
Doth every beast keep holiday;—
Thou child of joy,
Shout round me, let me hear thy shouts, thou happy
shepherd-boy !

IV.

Ye blessed creatures, I have heard the call
    Ye to each other make ; I see
The heavens laugh with you in your jubilee ;
    My heart is at your festival,
    My head hath its coronal,
The fulness of your bliss I feel—I feel it all.
    O evil day ! if I were sullen
    While Earth herself is adorning,
      This sweet May-morning,
    And the children are culling
      On every side,
    In a thousand valleys far and wide,
    Fresh flowers ; while the sun shines warm,
And the babe leaps up on his mother's arm :—
    I hear, I hear, with joy I hear !
    —But there's a tree, of many, one,
A single field which I have looked upon,
Both of them speak of something that is gone :
    The pansy at my feet
    Doth the same tale repeat :
Whither is fled the visionary gleam ?
Where is it now, the glory and the dream ?

V.

Our birth is but a sleep and a forgetting :
The Soul that rises with us, our life's Star,
    Hath had elsewhere its setting,
      And cometh from afar :
    Not in entire forgetfulness,
    And not in utter nakedness,

But trailing clouds of glory do we come
      From God, who is our home :
Heaven lies about us in our infancy !
Shades of the prison-house begin to close
      Upon the growing boy,
But he beholds the light, and whence it flows,
      He sees it in his joy ;
The youth, who daily farther from the East
      Must travel, still is Nature's priest,
      And by the vision splendid
      Is on his way attended ;
At length the man perceives it die away,
And fade into the light of common day.

VI.

Earth fills her lap with pleasures of her own ;
Yearnings she hath in her own natural kind,
And, even with something of a mother's mind,
      And no unworthy aim,
      The homely nurse doth all she can
To make her foster-child, her inmate Man,
      Forget the glories he hath known,
And that imperial palace whence he came.

VII.

Behold the Child among his new-born blisses,
A six-years' darling of a pigmy size !
See, where 'mid work of his own hand he lies,
Fretted by sallies of his mother's kisses,
With light upon him from his father's eyes !
See, at his feet, some little plan or chart,
Some fragment from his dream of human life,

Shaped by himself with newly-learned art ;
    A wedding or a festival,
    A mourning or a funeral ;
      And this hath now his heart,
    And unto this he frames his song :
      Then will he fit his tongue
To dialogues of business, love, or strife ;
    But it will not be long
    Ere this be thrown aside,
    And with new joy and pride
The little actor cons another part ;
Filling from time to time his ' humorous stage '
With all the Persons, down to palsied Age,
That Life brings with her in her equipage ;
    As if his whole vocation
    Were endless imitation.

VIII.

Thou, whose exterior semblance doth belie
    Thy soul's immensity ;
Thou best philosopher, who yet dost keep
Thy heritage, thou eye among the blind,
That, deaf and silent, read'st the eternal deep,
Haunted for ever by the eternal Mind.—
    Mighty Prophet ! Seer blest !
    On whom those truths do rest,
Which we are toiling all our lives to find,
In darkness lost, the darkness of the grave :
Thou, over whom thy Immortality
Broods like the day, a master o'er a slave,
A Presence which is not to be put by ;

R

Thou little child, yet glorious in the might
Of heaven-born freedom on thy being's height,
Why with such earnest pains dost thou provoke
The years to bring the inevitable yoke,
Thus blindly with thy blessedness at strife ?
Full soon thy soul shall have her earthly freight,
And custom lie upon thee with a weight,
Heavy as frost, and deep almost as life !

IX.

O joy ! that in our embers
Is something that doth live,
That Nature yet remembers
What was so fugitive !
The thought of our past years in me doth breed
Perpetual benediction : not indeed
For that which is most worthy to be blest—
Delight and liberty, the simple creed
Of childhood, whether busy or at rest, .
With new-fledged hope still fluttering in his breast :—
Not for these I raise
The song of thanks and praise :
But for those obstinate questionings
Of sense and outward things,
Fallings from us, vanishings ;
Blank misgivings of a creature
Moving about in worlds not realized ;
High instincts before which our mortal nature
Did tremble like a guilty thing surprised :
But for those first affections,
Those shadowy recollections,

Which, be they what they may,
Are yet the fountain-light of all our day,
Are yet a master light of all our seeing,
Uphold us, cherish, and have power to make
Our noisy years seem moments in the being
Of the eternal silence : truths that wake,
To perish never ;
Which neither listlessness, nor mad endeavour,
Nor man, nor boy,
Nor all that is at enmity with joy,
Can utterly abolish or destroy !
Hence, in a season of calm weather,
Though inland far we be,
Our souls have sight of that immortal sea
Which brought us hither ;
Can in a moment travel thither,
And see the children sport upon the shore,
And hear the mighty waters rolling evermore.

X.

Then sing, ye birds, sing, sing a joyous song !
And let the young lambs bound
As to the tabor's sound !
We in thought will join your throng,
Ye that pipe, and ye that play,
Ye that through your hearts to-day
Feel the gladness of the May !
What though the radiance which was once so bright
Be now for ever taken from my sight,
Though nothing can bring back the hour
Of splendour in the grass, of glory in the flower ;

We will grieve not, rather find
Strength in what remains behind ;
In the primal sympathy
Which having been must ever be ;
In the soothing thoughts that spring
Out of human suffering ;
In the faith that looks through death,
In years that bring the philosophic mind.

XI.

And oh, ye fountains, meadows, hills, and groves,
Forebode not any severing of our loves !
Yet in my heart of hearts I feel your might ;
I only have relinquished one delight
To live beneath your more habitual sway.
I love the brooks which down their channels fret,
Even more than when I tripped lightly as they ;
The innocent brightness of a new-born day
     Is lovely yet ;
· The clouds that gather round the setting sun
Do take a sober colouring from an eye
That hath kept watch o'er man's mortality ;
Another race hath been, and other palms are won.
Thanks to the human heart by which we live,
Thanks to its tenderness, its joys and fears,
To me the meanest flower that blows can give
Thoughts that do often lie too deep for tears.

WILLIAM WORDSWORTH.

BOOK III

DEATH AND IMMORTALITY.

Death and Immortality.

BEYOND THE VEIL.

THEY are all gone into the world of light,
   And I alone sit lingering here ;
Their very memory is fair and bright,
   And my sad thoughts doth clear.

It glows and glitters in my cloudy breast
   Like stars upon some gloomy grove,
Or those faint beams in which this hill is drest
   After the sun's remove.

I see them walking in an air of glory
   Whose light doth trample on my days—
My days, which are at best but dull and hoary,
   Mere glimmerings and decays.

O holy Hope and high Humility !
   High as the heavens above !
These are your walks, and you have showed them me
   To kindle my cold love.

Dear, beauteous Death! the jewel of the just!
  Shining nowhere but in the dark;
What mysteries do lie beyond thy dust,
  Could man outlook that mark!

He that hath found some fledged bird's nest may know,
  At first sight, if the bird be flown;
But what fair well or grove he sings in now,
  That is to him unknown.

And yet, as angels in some brighter dreams
  Call to the soul when man doth sleep,
So some strange thoughts transcend our wonted themes,
  And into glory peep.

If a star were confined into a tomb,
  Her captive flames must needs burn there:
But, when the hand that locked her up gives room,
  She'll shine through all the sphere.

O Father of eternal life, and all
  Created glories under Thee!
Resume thy spirit from this world of thrall
  Into true liberty.

Either disperse these mists, which blot and fill
  My perspective still as they pass;
Or else remove me hence unto that hill
  Where I shall need no glass.

HENRY VAUGHAN.

TIME'S BOOK.

AS Time one day by me did pass,
    Through a large dusky glass
He held, I chanced to look,
   And spied his curious book
Of past days, where sad Heaven did shed
A mourning light upon the dead.

Many disordered lives I saw,
    And foul records, which thaw
    My kind eyes still ; but in
    A fair, white page of thin
And even, smooth lines, like the sun's rays,
Thy name was writ and all thy days.

O bright and happy kalendar !
    Where youth shines like a star,
    All pearled with tears, and may
    Teach age the holy way ;
Where, through thick pangs, high agonies,
Faith into life breaks, and death dies.

As some meek night-piece which day quails,
    To candle-light unveils,
    So, by one beamy line
    From thy bright lamp, did shine,
In the same page, thy humble grave
Set with green herbs, glad hopes and brave.

Here slept my thought's dear mark ! which dust
    Seemed to devour like rust ;
    But dust, I did observe,
    By hiding doth preserve ;
As we, for long and sure recruits,
Candy with sugar our choice fruits.

O calm and sacred bed, where lies,
    In death's dark mysteries,
    A beauty far more bright
    Than the noon's cloudless light !
For whose dry dust green branches bud,
And robes are bleached in the Lamb's blood.

Sleep, happy ashes !—blessed sleep !
    While hapless I still weep ;
    Weep that I have out-lived
    My life, and unrelieved
Must, soulless shadow, so live on,
Though life be dead, and my joys gone.

                              HENRY VAUGHAN.

CONSOLATIONS IN BEREAVEMENT.

DEATH was full urgent with thee, Sister dear,
        And startling in his speed ;—
Brief pain, then languor till thy end came near—
        Such was the path decreed,
        The hurried road
To lead thy soul from earth to thine own God's abode.

Death wrought with thee, sweet maid, impatiently :—
      Yet merciful the haste
That baffles sickness ;—dearest, thou didst die ;
      Thou wast not made to taste
      Death's bitterness,
Decline's slow-wasting charm, or fever's fierce distress.

Death came unheralded :—but it was well ;
      For so thy Saviour bore
Kind witness, thou wast meet at once to dwell
      On his eternal shore ;
      All warning spared,
For none He gives where hearts are for prompt
    change prepared.

Death wrought in mystery; both complaint and cure
      To human skill unknown :—
God put aside all means, to make us sure
      It was his deed alone ;
      Lest we should lay
Reproach on our poor selves, that thou wast caught
    away.

Death urged as scant of time :—lest, Sister dear,
      We many a lingering day
Had sickened with alternate hope and fear,
      The ague of delay,
      Watching each spark
Of promise quenched in turn, till all our sky was dark.

Death came and went :—that so thy image might
    Our yearning hearts possess,
Associate with all pleasant thoughts and bright,
    With youth and loveliness ;
        Sorrow can claim,
Mary, nor lot nor part in thy soft soothing name.

Joy of sad hearts, and light of downcast eyes !
    Dearest, thou art enshrined
In all thy fragrance in our memories ;
    For we must ever find
        Bare thought of thee
Freshen this weary life, while weary life shall be.

                JOHN HENRY NEWMAN.

THE DESERTED HOUSE.

LIFE and Thought have gone away
    Side by side,
      Leaving door and windows wide :
Careless tenants they !

All within is dark as night :
In the windows is no light ;
And no murmur at the door,
So frequent on its hinge before.

Close the door, the shutters close,
    Or thro' the windows we shall see
      The nakedness and vacancy
Of the dark deserted house.

Come away : no more of mirth
  Is here, or merry-making sound.
The house was builded of the earth,
  And shall fall again to ground.

Come away ; for Life and Thought
  Here no longer dwell :
    But in a city glorious—
A great and distant city—have bought
  A mansion incorruptible.
    Would they could have stayed with us.

ALFRED TENNYSON.

FEAR OF DEATH.

SINCE Nature's works be good, and death doth
    serve
  As Nature's work, why should we fear to die ?
Since fear is vain but when it may preserve,
  Why should we fear that which we cannot fly ?
Fear is more pain than is the pain it fears,
  Disarming human minds of native might ;
While each conceit an ugly figure bears
  Which were not evil, well viewed in reason's light.
Our owly eyes, which dimmed with passions be,
  And scarce discern the dawn of coming day,
Let them be cleared, and now begin to see
  Our life is but a step in dusty way.
Then let us hold the bliss of peaceful mind ;
Since this we feel, great loss we cannot find.

SIR PHILIP SIDNEY.

GIVE PARDON, BLESSED SOUL.

GIVE pardon, blessed soul, to my bold cries,
    If they, importune, interrupt thy song
Which now, with joyful notes, thou sing'st among
The angel-quiristers of th' heavenly skies.
Give pardon, eke, sweet soul, to my slow cries,
    That since I saw thee now it is so long,
    And yet the tears that unto thee belong
To thee as yet they did not sacrifice.
I did not know that thou wert dead before,
    I did not feel the grief I did sustain :
The greater stroke astonisheth the more ;
    Astonishment takes from us sense of pain.
I stood amazed when others' tears begun,
And now begin to weep when they have done.

HENRY CONSTABLE.

DEATH, BE NOT PROUD.

DEATH ! be not proud, though some have callèd
    thee
Mighty and dreadful, for thou art not so ;
For those whom thou think'st thou dost overthrow
Die not, poor Death ! nor yet canst thou kill me.
From rest and sleep, which but thy picture be,
    Much pleasure ; then from thee much more must flow ;
    And soonest our best men with thee do go,
Rest of their bones, and soul's delivery.

Thou'rt slave to fate, chance, kings and desperate
    men,
  And dost with poison, war, and sickness dwell;
  And poppy or charms can make us sleep as well,
And better than thy stroke. Why swell'st thou then?
  One short sleep past, we wake eternally,
  And Death shall be no more : Death, thou shalt die!

JOHN DONNE.

SWEET DEATH.

THE sweetest blossoms die.
    And so it was that, going day by day
    Unto the church to praise and pray,
And crossing the green churchyard thoughtfully,
    I saw how on the graves the flowers
    Shed their fresh leaves in showers,
And how their perfume rose up to the sky
    Before it passed away.

The youngest blossoms die.
    They die, and fall, and nourish the rich earth
    From which they lately had their birth;
Sweet life, but sweeter death that passeth by
    And is as though it had not been :—
    All colours turn to green;
The bright hues vanish and the odours fly,
    The grass hath lasting worth.

And youth and beauty die.
  So be it, O my God, Thou God of truth :
  Better than beauty and than youth
Are Saints and Angels, a glad company;
  And Thou, O Lord, our Rest and Ease,
  Art better far than these.
Why should we shrink from our full harvest ? Why
  Prefer to glean with Ruth ?

CHRISTINA ROSSETTI.

NIGHT AND DEATH.

M YSTERIOUS Night! When our first parent
    knew   ,
Thee from report divine and heard thy name,
Did he not tremble for this lovely frame,
This glorious canopy of light and blue ?
Yet 'neath a curtain of translucent dew,
Bathed in the rays of the great setting flame,
Hesperus with the host of heaven came ;
And lo ! Creation widened in man's view.
Who could have thought such darkness lay concealed
Within thy beams, O Sun ! Or who could find,
Whilst fly and leaf and insect stood revealed,
That to such countless orbs thou mad'st us blind ?
Why do we, then, shun death with anxious strife ?
If Light can thus deceive, wherefore not Life?

JOSEPH BLANCO WHITE.

DESIDERIA.

SURPRISED by joy—impatient as the wind
　I turned to share the transport—Oh! with whom
But Thee, deep buried in the silent tomb,
That spot which no vicissitude can find?
Love, faithful love, recalled thee to my mind—
But how could I forget thee? Through what power,
Even for the least division of an hour,
Have I been so beguiled as to be blind
To my most grievous loss?—That thought's return
Was the worst pang that sorrow ever bore,
Save one, one only, when I stood forlorn,
Knowing my heart's best treasure was no more;
That neither present time, nor years unborn,
Could to my sight that heavenly face restore.

WILLIAM WORDSWORTH.

THE LULLABY.

I SAW two children hushed to death,
　In lap of One with silver wings,
Hearkening a lute, whose latest breath
　Low lingered on the trembling strings.

Her face is very pale and fair,
　Her hooded eyelids darkly shed
Celestial love, and all her hair
　Is like a crown around her head.

S

Each ripple sinking in its place,
 Along the lute's faint-ebbing strain,
Seems echoed slowlier from her face,
 And echoed back from theirs again.

Yes, now is silence. Do not weep.
 Her eyes are fixed ; observe them long ;
And spell, if thou canst pierce so deep,
 The purpose of a nobler song.

WILLIAM ALLINGHAM.

FIRE.

SWEET maiden, for so calm a life
 Too bitter seemed thine end ;
But thou had'st won thee, ere that strife,
 A more than earthly friend.

We miss thee in thy place at school,
 And on thine homeward way,
Where violets by the reedy pool,
 Peep out so shyly gay ;

Where thou, a true and gentle guide,
 Would'st lead thy little band,
With all an elder sister's pride,
 And rule with eye and hand.

And if *we* miss, O who may speak
 What thoughts are hovering round
The pallet where thy fresh young cheek
 Its evening slumber found ?

How many a tearful longing look
   In silence seeks thee yet,
Where, in its own familiar nook,
   Thy fireside chair is set?

And oft when little voices dim
   Are feeling for the note
In chanted prayer, or psalm, or hymn,
   And wavering wildly float,

Comes gushing o'er a sudden thought
   Of her who led the strain,
How oft such music home she brought—
   But ne'er shall bring again.

O say not so, the spring-tide air
   Is fraught with whisperings sweet;
Who knows but heavenly carols there
   With ours may duly meet?

Who knows how near, each holy hour,
   The pure and child-like dead
May linger, where, in shrine or bower,
   The mourner's prayer is said?

And He who willed thy tender frame
   (O stern, yet sweet decree!)
Should wear the martyr's robe of flame,
   He hath prepared for thee

A garland in that region bright
   Where infant spirits reign,
Tinged faintly with such golden light
   As crowns his martyr train.

Nay, doubt it not : his tokens sure
  Were round her death-bed shown :
The wasting pain might not endure,
  'Twas calm ere life had flown,

Even as we read of saints of yore :
  Her heart and voice were free
To crave one quiet slumber more
  Upon her mother's knee.

JOHN KEBLE.

ON THE DEATH OF TWO LITTLE CHILDREN.

AH ! bitter chance ! no arm the blow could ward,
    Or shield from hurt her guileless infant breast,
New to this perilous world, and daily prest
To a fond mother's heart ; her lot looks hard ;
But lo ! her face is calm—a gentle tone
Seems murmuring from those lips that breathe no
    more,
'Come, little sister, marked for heaven before,
I crave that hand yet smaller than mine own,
That baby-hand to clasp again in mine !'
Sweet spirit ! as thou wishest it shall be ;
Death drops his wing on younger heads than thine,
Though thine is of the youngest ; soon to thee
The little sister of thy soul shall come,
And one low funeral bell shall bring ye home.

CHARLES TURNER.

ON AN INFANT,

WHICH DIED BEFORE BAPTISM.

' BE, rather than be called, a child of God !'
  Death whispered ;—with assenting nod,
Its head upon its mother's breast
The baby bowed, without demur—
Of the kingdom of the Blest
Possessor, not inheritor.

SAMUEL TAYLOR COLERIDGE.

THE DEATH OF BABE CHRISTABEL.

WITH her white hands claspt she sleepeth ; heart
  is husht and lips are cold ;
Death shrouds up her heaven of beauty, and a
  weary way I go,
Like the sheep without a shepherd on the wintry
  norland wold
With the face of day shut out by blinding snow.

O'er its widowed nest my heart sits moaning for its
  young that's fled
From this world of wail and weeping, gone to join
  her starry peers ;
And my light of life's o'ershadowed where the dear
  one lieth dead,
And I'm crying in the dark with many fears.

All last night-tide she seemed near me, like a lost
    belovèd bird,
  Beating at the lattice louder than the sobbing wind
    and rain ;
And I called across the night with tender name and
    fondling word ;
  And I yearned out thro' the darkness, all in vain.

Heart will plead, 'Eyes cannot see her : they are
    blind with tears of pain ;'
  And it climbeth up and straineth, for dear life, to
    look and hark
While I call her once again : but there cometh no
    refrain,
  And it droppeth down, and dieth in the dark.

In this dim world of clouding cares,
    We rarely know, till wildered eyes
    See white wings lessening up the skies,
The Angels with us unawares.

And thou hast stolen a jewel, Death !
    Shall light thy dark up like a star,
    A Beacon kindling from afar
Our light of love, and fainting faith.

Thro' tears it gleams perpetually,
    And glitters thro' the thickest glooms, ·
    Till the eternal morning comes
To light us o'er the Jasper Sea.

With our best branch in tenderest leaf,
   We've strewn the way our Lord doth come ;
   And, ready for the harvest-home,
His Reapers bind our ripest sheaf.

Our beautiful Bird of light hath fled :
   Awhile she sat with folded wings,
   Sang round us a few hoverings,
Then straightway into glory sped.

And white-winged Angels nurture her ;
   With heaven's white radiance robed and crowned,
   And all Love's purple glory round,
She summers on the Hills of Myrrh.

Through childhood's morning-land, serene
   She walkt betwixt us twain, like Love ;
   While, in a robe of light above,
Her better Angel walkt unseen,

Till Life's highway broke bleak and wild ;
   Then, lest her starry garments trail
   In mire, heart bleed, and courage fail,
The Angel's arms caught up the child.

Her wave of life hath backward rolled
   To the great ocean, on whose shore
   We wander up and down to store
Some treasures of the times of old :

And aye we seek and hunger on
   For precious pearls and relics rare
   Strewn on the sands for us to wear
At heart, for love of her that's gone.

O weep no more ! there yet is balm
   In Gilead ! Love doth ever shed
   Rich healing where it nestles,—spread
O'er desert pillows some green palm !

Strange glory streams thro' Life's wild rents,
   And thro' the open door of Death
   We see the heaven that beckoneth
To the Belovèd going hence.

God's ichor fills the hearts that bleed ;
   The best fruit loads the broken bough ;
   And in the wounds our sufferings plough
Immortal Love sows sovereign seed.

                 GERALD MASSEY.

EVELYN HOPE.

BEAUTIFUL Evelyn Hope is dead !
   Sit and watch by her side an hour.
That is her book-shelf, this her bed ;
   She plucked that piece of geranium-flower,
Beginning to die too, in the glass ;
   Little has yet been changed, I think :
The shutters are shut, no light may pass
   Save two long rays thro' the hinges' chink.

Sixteen years old when she died !
   Perhaps she had scarcely heard my name ;
It was not her time to love ; beside,
   Her life had many a hope and aim,
Duties enough and little cares,
   And now was quiet, now astir,
Till God's hand beckoned unawares,—
   And the sweet white brow is all of her.

Is it too late then, Evelyn Hope ?
   What, your soul was pure and true,
The good stars met in your horoscope,
   Made you of spirit, fire and dew—
And, just because I was thrice as old
   And our paths in the world diverged so wide,
Each was nought to each, must I be told ?
   We were fellow mortals, nought beside ?

No, indeed ! for God above
   Is great to grant, as mighty to make,
And creates the love to reward the love :
   I claim you still, for my own love's sake !
Delayed it may be for more lives yet,
   Through worlds I shall traverse, not a few :
Much is to learn, and much to forget,
   Ere the time be come for taking you.

But the time will come,—at last it will,
   When, Evelyn Hope, what meant (I shall say)
In the lower earth, in the years long still,
   That body and soul so pure and gay ?

Why your hair was amber, I shall divine,
  And your mouth of your own geranium's red—
And what you would do with me, in fine,
  In the new life come in the old one's stead.

I have lived (I shall say) so much since then,
  Given up myself so many times,
Gained me the gains of various men,
  Ransacked the ages, spoiled the climes;
Yet one thing, one, in my soul's full scope,
  Either I missed or itself missed me:
And I want and find you, Evelyn Hope!
  What is the issue? let us see!

I loved you, Evelyn, all the while!
  My heart seemed full as it could hold—
There was place and to spare for the frank young smile,
  And the red young mouth, and the hair's young gold.
So, hush,—I will give you this leaf to keep:
  See, I shut it inside the sweet cold hand!
There, that is our secret: go to sleep!
  You will wake, and remember, and understand.

ROBERT BROWNING.

GONE.

A NOTHER hand is beckoning us,
  Another call is given,
And glows once more with angel-steps
  The path which reaches Heaven.

Our young and gentle friend, whose smile
    Made brighter summer hours,
Amid the frosts of autumn time
    Has left us, with the flowers.

No paling of the cheek of bloom
    Forewarned us of decay ;
No shadow from the Silent Land
    Fell round our sister's way.

The light of her young life went down,
    As sinks behind the hill
The glory of a setting star—
    Clear, suddenly, and still.

As pure and sweet, her fair brow seemed
    Eternal as the sky ;
And like the brook's low song, her voice,—
    A sound which could not die.

And half we deemed she needed not
    The changing of her sphere,
To give to Heaven a Shining One,
    Who walked an Angel here.

The blessing of her quiet life
    Fell on us like the dew ;
And good thoughts, where her footsteps pressed,
    Like fairy blossoms grew.

Sweet promptings unto kindest deeds
  Were in her very look ;
We read her face, as one who reads
  A true and holy book ;

The measure of a blessed hymn,
  To which our hearts could move ;
The breathing of an inward psalm ;
  A canticle of love.

We miss her in the place of prayer,
  And by the hearth-fire's light ;
We pause beside her door to hear
  Once more her sweet ' Good-night !'

There seems a shadow on the day
  Her smile no longer cheers ;
A dimness on the stars of night,
  Like eyes that look through tears.

Alone unto our Father's will
  One thought hath reconciled—
That He whose love exceedeth ours
  Hath taken home his child.

Fold her, O Father ! in thine arms,
  And let her henceforth be
A messenger of love between
  Our human hearts and Thee.

Still let her mild rebuking stand
  Between us and the wrong,

And her dear memory serve to make
  Our faith in goodness strong.

And grant that she who, trembling, here
  Distrusted all her powers,
May welcome to her holier home
  The well-beloved of ours.

JOHN GREENLEAF WHITTIER.

THE DEATH-BED.

WE watched her breathing through the night,
  Her breathing soft and low,
As in her breast the wave of life
  Kept heaving to and fro.

So silently we seemed to speak,
  So slowly moved about,
As we had lent her half our powers
  To eke her living out.

Our very hopes belied our fears,
  Our fears our hopes belied—
We thought her dying when she slept,
  And sleeping when she died.

For when the morn came dim and sad,
  And chill with early showers,
Her quiet eyelids closed—she had
  Another morn than ours.

THOMAS HOOD.

RELEASED.

A LITTLE, low-ceiled room.   Four walls
   Whose blank shut out all else of life,
And crowded close within their bound
   A world of pain and toil and strife.

Her world.   Scarce furthermore she knew
   Of God's great globe that wondrously
Outrolls a glory of green earth,
   And frames it with the restless sea.

Four closer walls of common pine ;
   And therein lying, cold and still,
The weary flesh that long hath borne
   Its patient mystery of ill.

Regardless now of work to do,
   No queen more careless in her state,
Hands crossed in an unbroken calm ;
   For other hands the work may wait.

Put by her implements of toil,
   Put by each coarse, intrusive sign ;
She made a Sabbath when she died,
   And round her breathes a rest divine.

Put by, at last, beneath the lid,
   The exempted hands, the tranquil face ;
Uplift her in her dreamless sleep,
   And bear her gently from the place.

Oft she hath gazed, with wistful eyes,
  Out from that threshold on the night;
The narrow bourn she crosseth now;
  She standeth in the eternal light.

Oft she hath pressed, with aching feet,
  Those broken steps that reach the door;
Henceforth, with angels, she shall tread
  Heaven's golden stair, for evermore!

ADELINE D. T. WHITNEY.

SONNET.

I CANNOT think that thou shouldst pass away,
  Whose life to mine is an eternal law,
A piece of nature that can have no flaw,
A new and certain sunrise every day.
But, if thou art to be another ray
About the Sun of Life, and art to live
Free from all of thee that was fugitive,
The debt of love I will more fully pay,—
Not downcast with the thought of thee so high,
But, rather, raised to be a nobler man,
And more divine in my humanity;
As knowing that the waiting eyes which scan
My life, are lighted by a purer being,
And ask meek, calm-browed deeds, with it agreeing.

JAMES RUSSELL LOWELL.

SOUL OF MY FRIEND.

SOUL of my Friend ! if in thy heavenly rest
    Thou dost our earthly turmoil still survey,
And whom thou lovedst ere thou went'st away
Them lovest yet, be with me, spirit blest !
If not in presence, yet in power confest.
For I am sorely tried in this my day,
And almost—but I know not what I say—
Almost could doubt if all be for the best.
Come, therefore, thou, with purgèd insight wise,
Interpret me the good of all these fears ;
This burning under which my spirit lies—
Is it the brand which heals, or that which sears?
O God ! I see a trembling in thine eyes,
As when deep joy falls back, disdaining tears.

THOMAS BURBIDGE.

BURIAL OF THE DEAD.

I THOUGHT to meet no more, so dreary seemed
    Death's interposing veil, and thou so pure,
        Thy place in Paradise
        Beyond where I could soar,

Friend of this worthless heart !   But happier thoughts
Spring, like unbidden violets, from the sod,
        Where patiently thou tak'st
        Thy sweet and sure repose.

The shadows fall more soothing : the soft air
Is full of cheering whispers like thine own ;
  While Memory, by thy grave,
  Lives o'er thy funeral day ;

The deep knell dying down, the mourners' pause
Waiting their Saviour's welcome at the gate.—
  Sure with the words of Heaven
  Thy spirit met us there,

And sought with us along the accustomed way
The hallowed porch, and, entering in, beheld
  The pageant of sad joy,
  So dear to Faith and Hope.

O ! hadst thou brought a strain from Paradise
To cheer us, happy soul, thou hadst not touched
  The sacred springs of grief
  More tenderly and true,

Than those deep-warbled anthems, high and low,
Low as the grave, high as the Eternal Throne,
  Guiding, through light and gloom,
  Our mourning fancies wild,

Till gently, like soft golden clouds at eve
Around the western twilight, all subside
  Into a placid Faith,
  That even with beaming eye

Counts thy sad honours, coffin, bier, and pall ;
So many relics of a frail love lost,
  So many tokens dear
  Of endless love begun.

      T

Listen ! it is no dream : the Apostle's trump
Gives earnest of the Archangel's ; calmly now,
    Our hearts yet beating high
    To that victorious lay,

Most like a warrior's to the martial dirge
Of a true comrade, in the grave we trust
    Our treasure for a while :
    And if a tear steal down,

If human anguish o'er the shaded brow
Pass shuddering, when the handful of pure earth
    Touches the coffin lid :
    If at our brother's name

Once and again the thought, 'for ever gone,'
Come o'er us like a cloud ; yet, gentle spright,
    Thou turnest not away,
    Thou knowest us calm at heart.

One look, and we have seen our last of thee
Till we too sleep and our long sleep be o'er :
    O cleanse us, ere we view
    That countenance pure again,

Thou who canst change the heart, and raise the
    dead !
As Thou art by to soothe our parting hour,
    Be ready when we meet;
    With thy dear pardoning words.

John Keble.

GUIDING STARS.

J OY of my life while left me here;
     And still my Love!
How in thy absence thou dost steer
     Me from above!
     A life well led   '
     This truth commends;
     With quick or dead
     It never ends.

Stars are of mighty use. The night
     Is dark and long;
The road foul; and where one goes right
     Six may go wrong.
     One twinkling ray,
     Shot o'er some cloud,
     May clear much way
     And guide a crowd.

God's saints are shining lights: who stays
     Here long must pass
O'er dark hills, swift streams, and steep ways
     As smooth as glass;
     But these all night
     Like candles shed
     Their beams, and light
     Us into bed.

They are indeed our pillar-fires,
    Seen as we go ;
They are that city's shining spires
    We travel to.
    A sword-like gleam
    Kept man for sin
    First *out :* this beam
    Will guide him *in.*

             HENRY VAUGHAN.

SONNET.

RIVER that stealest with such silent pace
    Around the City of the Dead, where lies
A friend who bore thy name, and whom these eyes
Shall see no more in his accustomed place,
Linger and fold him in thy soft embrace
    And say good-night ; for now the western skies
    Are red with sunset, and grey mists arise
    Like damps that gather on a dead man's face.
Good-night ! good-night ! as we so oft have said
    Beneath this roof at midnight, in the days
    That are no more, and shall no more return.
Thou hast but taken thy lamp and gone to bed :
    I stay a little longer, as one stays
    To cover up the embers that still burn.

        HENRY WADSWORTH LONGFELLOW.

CONSOLATION.

ALL are not taken : there are left behind
   Living Belovèds, tender looks to bring,
And make the daylight still a happy thing,
And tender voices to make soft the wind.
But if it were not so—if I could find
No love in all the world for comforting,
Nor any path but hollowly did ring,
Where 'dust to dust' the love from life disjoined,
And if, before those sepulchres unmoving
I stood alone (as some forsaken lamb
Goes bleating up the moors in weary dearth)
Crying 'Where are ye, O my loved and loving?'—
I know a Voice would sound, 'Daughter, I AM.
Can I suffice for Heaven, and not for Earth?'

ELIZABETH BARRETT BROWNING.

AFTER MY SISTER'S DEATH.

THE westering sun in copious floods
   Pours thick his slanting beams,
Fair show the shining eastern woods,
   And fair the glancing streams.

Just such another glittering scene,
   And just a year gone by,
As if no time did intervene,
   Met my rejoicing eye.

Spring with loose hand rich gifts did share
  Through her advancing realm ;
White showed the bloom upon the pear,
  And green the bursting elm.

Cheerly the thrush with broken notes
  Did give the day adieu ;
And through the trees the red-tiled cotes
  Broke brightly into view.

Just such another spring so fast
  Repairs the earth again,
But, oh, a brighter spring is past
  I never shall regain.

Spring of my soul ! my being's May,
  Departed, and for ever !
There is no voice but speaks to say
  For ever and for ever !

The sun's hot rays may soon unloose
  Pale winter's frozen grasp,
New life in Nature soon induce
  The warm air's circling clasp.

But what reviving summer sun
  Shall thaw thy hand, O Death ?
Or breezy south, when once 'tis flown,
  Restore the stolen breath ?

What ! shall the faithful God, who leads
  The long revolving year,—
Who in his bosom warms the seeds,
  And breathes on Nature's bier,—

Let lapse in earth our mortal goal—
    This life, our seed immortal?
Or this diviner spring—our soul,
    Let freeze in Death's cold portal!

It may not, and it cannot be!
    Cease, doubtful, trembling heart!
Trust then thy God, nor doubt that she
    Survives, not far apart.

WILLIAM CALDWELL ROSCOE.

TO A FRIEND.

SAD soul, whom God, resuming what He gave,
    Medicines with bitter anguish of the tomb,
Cease to oppress the portals of the grave,
And strain thy aching sight across the gloom.
The surged Atlantic's winter-beaten wave
Shall sooner pierce the purpose of the wind,
Than thy storm-tost and heavy-swelling mind
Grasp the full import of his means to save.
Through the dark night lie still; God's faithful grace
Lies hid, like morning, underneath the sea.
Let thy slow hours roll, like these weary stars,
Down to the level ocean patiently;
Till his loved hand shall touch the eastern bars,
And his full glory shine upon thy face.

WILLIAM CALDWELL ROSCOE.

'How is it ?   Canst thou feel for me
Some painless sympathy with pain ?'

In Memoriam.

WHY fear that the departed grieves,
    Far from the mourner whom she leaves?
Who shall deny that when he stands,
With aching breast and strainèd hands,
His wan face raised to empty air,
And his hopes darkening to despair,—

E'en then the spirit whom he loved,
By close affection deeply moved,
Comes, with a swift angelic grace,
And gazes on the dear loved face,
Yearns to wipe off the raining tears
And whisper comfort in his ears ?

Or rather, from beyond the flood
Leaning her young beatitude,
Sighs only gently to behold
How grief's sharp fires transmute her gold,
And, rich in insight newly given,
Counts every faltering step to Heaven ?

Rests tenderly a soft distress
Upon the coming happiness :
And, blest to think how short a time
Severs these frosts from golden prime,
Smiles as a mother smiles to trace
Brief showers roll down her baby's face.

WILLIAM CALDWELL ROSCOE.

A VOICE FROM AFAR.

WEEP not for me ;—
　　Be blithe as wont, nor tinge with gloom
The stream of love that circles home,
　　Light hearts and free !
Joy in the gifts Heaven's bounty lends ;
　　Nor miss my face, dear friends !

　　I still am near ;—
Watching the smiles I prized on earth,
Your converse mild, your blameless mirth ;
　　Now too I hear
Of whispered sounds the tale complete,
　　Low prayers, and musings sweet.

　　A sea before
The Throne is spread ; its pure, still glass
Pictures all earth scenes as they pass.
　　We, on its shore,
Share, in the bosom of our rest,
　　God's knowledge, and are blest !

　　　　　　　　　JOHN HENRY NEWMAN.

DIRGE.

KNOWS he who tills this lonely field
　　To reap its scanty corn,
What mystic fruit his acres yield
　　At midnight and at morn ?

In the long sunny afternoon
  The plain was full of ghosts ;
I wandered up, I wandered down,
  Beset by pensive hosts.

The winding Concord gleamed below,
  Pouring as wide a flood·
As when my brothers, long ago,
  Came with me to the wood.

But they are gone,—the holy ones
  Who trod with me this lovely vale,
The strong, star-bright companions
  Are silent, low, and pale.

My good, my noble, in their prime,
  Who made this world the feast it was,
Who learned with me the lore of time,
  Who loved this dwelling-place !

They took this valley for their toy,
  They played with it in every mood,
A cell for prayer, a hall for joy—
  They treated Nature as they would.

They coloured the horizon round,
  Stars flamed and faded as they bade,
All echoes hearkened for their sound,
  They made the woodlands glad or mad.

I touch this flower of silken leaf
  Which once our childhood knew;
Its soft leaves wound me with a grief
  Whose balsam never grew.

Hearken to yon pine warbler,
  Singing aloft in the tree !
Hearest thou, O traveller,
  What he singeth to me ?

Nôt unless God made sharp thine ear
  With sorrow such as mine,
Out of that delicate lay couldst thou
  Its heavy tale divine.

' Go, lonely man,' it saith,
  ' They loved thee from their birth ;
Their hands were pure, and pure their faith—
  There are no such hearts on earth.

' Ye drew one mother's milk,
  One chamber held ye all,
A very tender history
  Did in your childhood fall.

' Ye cannot unlock your heart,
  The key is gone with them ;
The silent organ loudest chants
  The master's requiem.'

RALPH WALDO EMERSON.

MY MOTHER.

(Portobello, near Edinburgh, 1851.)

THERE was a gathered stillness in the room,
  Only the breathing of the great sea rose
From far off, aiding that profound repose,
With regular pulse and pause within the gloom
Of twilight, as if some impending doom
  Was now approaching ;—I sat moveless there,
  Watching with tears and thoughts that were like
    prayer,
Till the hour struck,—the thread dropped from the
    loom,—
  And the Bark passed in which freed souls are borne.
  The dear stilled face lay there ; that sound forlorn
Continued ; I rose not, but long sat by :—
  And now my heart oft hears that sad seashore,
When she is in the far-off land, and I
  Wait the dark sail returning yet once more.

WILLIAM BELL SCOTT

MAY AND DEATH.

I WISH that when you died last May,
  Charles, there had died along with you
Three parts of spring's delightful things ;
  Ay, and, for me, the fourth part too.

A foolish thought, and worse, perhaps !
  There must be many a pair of friends

Who, arm in arm, deserve the warm
  Moon-births and the long evening-ends.

So, for their sake be May still May !
  Let their new time, as mine of old,
Do all it did for me : I bid
  Sweet sights and sounds throng manifold.

Only, one little sight, one plant,
  Woods have in May, that starts up green
Save a sole streak which, so to speak,
  Is spring's blood, spilt its leaves between,—

That, they might spare ; a certain wood
  Might miss the plant ; their loss were small :
But I,—whene'er the leaf grows there,
  Its drop comes from my heart, that's all.
                          ROBERT BROWNING.

AN ANNIVERSARY.

I.

TWO years ago, this day, he died ;
  In silence to the grave he stole ;
To many friends their joy and pride,—
  To me the brother of my soul.

Then died their hopes and were not seen,
  But still our love, it seems to me,
Survives, though something hangs between—
  A haze—a dim perplexity ;

Perplexity that gathers still
   Veil over veil, fold upon fold ;
Like mists of rain about a lonely hill
   Round me that cloud contracts or is unrolled.

Come often intimations, as it were,
   He still were somewhere dwelling on the earth ;
Some look that of his beauty hath a share,
   Some laugh that hath a sound of his delicious mirth

II.

If I no more behold thy face
   I know thou art not lost ; I know
Christ keeps thee in a safer place,
   And I at heart would have it so.

I murmur not.   O soul above,
   'Tis not my voice thou hearest groan ;
'Tis sin that counterfeits my love ;
   I but for weakness moan.

But no, thou hast a finer ear,
   And thou, I trust—'tis more than *I* dare say,—
Discern'st the joyful spirit singing clear
   Even in this miserable house of clay.

III.

Year after misty year comes forth,
   And old things flee and new arrive ;
And still he lingers on the earth—
   My friend is still alive.

Or if sometimes he be not here,
　　Like flowerets of the spring
Soon doth his beauty reappear,
　　A renovated thing.

Kin to all love and nobleness,
　　All glory is his heir;
No deed to praise, no sight to bless
　　Comes out, but he is there.

Is he alive in truth, or dead and dull,
　　And lost, for ever lost to mortal eye?
O friend, so noble and so beautiful,
　　While earth is fair, to me thou canst not die !

　　　　　　　　　　　THOMAS BURBIDGE.

DEAR FRIEND, FAR OFF.

DEAR friend, far off, my lost desire,
　　So far, so near, in woe and weal;
　　O loved the most when most I feel
There is a lower and a higher;

Known and unknown; human, divine;
　　Sweet human hand and lips and eye,
　　Dear heavenly friend that canst not die,
Mine, mine for ever, ever mine;

Strange friend, past, present, and to be;
  Loved deeplier, darklier understood;
  Behold, I dream a dream of good,
And mingle all the world with thee.

ALFRED TENNYSON.

HOW PURE AT HEART.

H OW pure at heart and sound in head,
    With what divine affections bold
    Should be the man whose thought would
    hold
An hour's communion with the dead.

In vain shalt thou, or any, call
  The spirits from their golden day,
  Except, like them, thou too canst say
My spirit is at peace with all.

They haunt the silence of the breast,
  Imaginations calm and fair,
  The memory like a cloudless air,
The conscience as a sea at rest:

But when the heart is full of din,
  And doubt beside the portal waits,
  They can but listen at the gates
And hear the household jar within.

ALFRED TENNYSON.

THE PROSPECT.

M ETHINKS we do as fretful children do,
　　Leaning their faces on the window-pane
To sigh the glass dim with their own breath's stain,
And shut the sky and landscape from their view :
And thus, alas, since God the Maker drew
A mystic separation 'twixt those twain,
The life beyond us, and our souls in pain,
We miss the prospect which we are called unto,
By grief we are fools to use.　Be still and strong,
O man, my brother ! hold thy sobbing breath,
And keep thy soul's large window pure from wrong ;
That so, as life's appointment issueth,
Thy vision may be clear to watch along
The sunset consummation-lights of death.

　　　　　　　　ELIZABETH BARRETT BROWNING.

SUSPIRIA.

T AKE them, O Death ! and bear away
　　Whatever thou canst call thine own !
Thine image, stamped upon this clay,
　　Doth give thee that, but that alone.

Take them, O Grave ! and let them lie.
　　Folded upon thy narrow shelves.
As garments by the soul laid by,
　　And precious only to ourselves.

U

Take them, O great Eternity !
Our little life is but a gust,
That bends the branches of thy tree
And trails its blossoms in the dust.

HENRY WADSWORTH LONGFELLOW.

O LIVING WILL.

O LIVING Will that shalt endure,
    When all that seems shall suffer shock,
    Rise in the spiritual rock,
Flow through our deeds and make them pure,

That we may lift from out of dust
    A cry as unto Him that hears,
    A cry above the conquered years,
To One that with us works, and trust,

With faith that comes of self-control,
    The truths that never can be proved
    Until we close with all we loved,
And all we flow from, soul in soul !

ALFRED TENNYSON.

NOTES.

----◆----

PAGE

6. MAY CAROLS.—The 2nd of Part I. and 10th of Part II. of the *May Carols.*

9. EVENTIDE.—The second part of the poem.

20. BY THE SEA.—I have ventured to restore the fifth line to the form in which the poet first published it.

41. TO A SKYLARK.—As originally published. The second stanza was afterwards transferred to the poem, *A Morning Exercise.*

53. THREE SONNETS.—From the series of *Coruisken Sonnets* in the *Book of Orm.*

60. THE RAINBOW.—The first part of the poem. In the tenth line Mr. Grosart's conjecture has been adopted, that " Forms," in the original, may be a misprint for " Storms."

69. THE RIGHT MUST WIN.—Nine stanzas omitted.

71. THE MANLY LIFE.—An extract from *Cupid's Conflict.*

78. GOOD LIFE.—The third strophe of the *Ode to the Immortal Memory and Friendship oj that Noble Pair Sir Lucius Cary and Sir Henry Morison.*

119. DRYNESS IN PRAYER.—One stanza omitted.

144. STRONG SON OF GOD.—The last three stanzas omitted.

148. THE WILL OF GOD.—Three stanzas omitted.

155. SOWING IN FAITH.—Sonnet addressed to the Rev. John Hamilton Thom.

161. LIFE STRUGGLES.—These two Sonnets are, with the author's consent, retained in the form and connexion in which they appeared in his *Poems by a Painter*, 1854.

163. THY WAY IS IN THE DEEP.—From *Hymns for the Christian Church and Home*. Edited by Rev. James Martineau.

192. THE STARRY SKIES.—One stanza omitted.

196. THE NIGHT.—The latter part of the poem.

217. TWO SONNETS.—See note to p. 53.

231. LIFE.—An extract from the original poem.

254. GIVE PARDON.—The first of four Sonnets addressed by Henry Constable to Sir Philip Sidney's Soul, prefixed to Sidney's Apology for Poetry, 1595.

260. DEATH OF TWO CHILDREN.—They were the daughters of the Hon. Gustavus and Lady Katharine Hamilton Russell, the eldest of whom died by an accident during the mortal illness of her sister, who almost immediately followed her. They were both buried on the same day.

261. DEATH OF BABE CHRISTABEL.—The last two sections of *The Ballad of Babe Christabel*.

276. SONNET.—From the five Sonnets entitled *Three Friends of Mine.*

INDEX OF AUTHORS.

PAGE

ALLINGHAM, WILLIAM, *b.* 1828 . . . 50, 83, 101, 103, 110, 112, 257

ARNOLD, MATTHEW, *b.* 1822 . 40, 74, 76, 107, 208, 225

AUSTIN, JOHN, *d.* 1669 117

BARBAULD, ANNA LÆTITIA (1743—1825) . . . 231

BROWNING, ELIZABETH BARRETT (1809—1861) . 29, 30, 81, 100, 101, 147, 177, 190, 202, 207, 215, 219, 277, 289

BROWNING, ROBERT, *b.* 1812 . . 199, 233, 264, 284

BRYANT, WILLIAM CULLEN, *b.* 1794 33

BUCHANAN, ROBERT, *b.* 1841 . . 53, 54, 55, 217, 218

BURBIDGE, THOMAS, *b.* 1816 . . 9, 135, 220, 272, 285

CHANNING, WILLIAM ELLERY, *b.* 1818 . . . 223

CLIVE, MRS. ARCHER (1801—1873) . . . 222, 229

CLOUGH, ARTHUR HUGH (1819—1861) 129, 145, 146, 166, 167, 169, 170, 213, 228

COLERIDGE, HARTLEY (1796—1849) . 57, 74, 115, 122, 123, 160, 171 186

COLERIDGE, SAMUEL TAYLOR (1772—1834) . 205, 261

CONSTABLE, HENRY (1555—1604) 254

CRANCH, CHRISTOPHER PEARSE, *b.* 1813 . . . 180

DE VERE, AUBREY, *b.* 1814 . . 6, 30, 43, 64, 147, 180

PAGE

DONNE, JOHN (1573—1631) 254
DRUMMOND, WILLIAM (1585—1649). . . . 27

EMERSON, RALPH WALDO, *b.* 1803 . . . . 14, 281

FABER, FREDERICK WILLIAM (1815—1863) . 69, 119, 124,
137, 148, 153, 192
FLETCHER, PHINEAS (1584—1650) 116

GRAY, DAVID (1838—1861) 54, 106
GREENWELL, DORA, *b.* 1821 . . . . . 56, 232

HERBERT, GEORGE (1593—1632) . 11, 62, 89, 90, 106,
134, 156
HERRICK, ROBERT (1591—1674) 52
HOOD, THOMAS (1798—1845) 269
HUNT, LEIGH (1784—1859) 183

INGELOW, JEAN, *b.* 1830 . . . . . 99, 185

JONSON, BEN (1574—1637) 78

KEBLE, JOHN (1792—1866) . . . 35, 36, 258, 272
KEMBLE, FRANCES ANNE, *b.* 1811 . . . 96, 168, 222
KINGSLEY, CHARLES (1819—1875) 82, 165

LONGFELLOW, HENRY WADSWORTH, *b.* 1807 42, 112, 211,
276, 289
LOWELL, JAMES RUSSELL, *b.* 1819 . 28, 77, 182, 187, 271

MACDONALD, GEORGE, *b.* 1824 . . . . 92, 97, 197
MARVELL, ANDREW (1620—1678) 61
MASSEY, GERALD, *b.* 1828 261
MILTON, JOHN (1608—1674) 72
MORE, HENRY (1614—1687) 71
MUNBY, ARTHUR, *pub.* 1865 . . . . . 59, 218

PAGE

NEWMAN, JOHN HENRY, *b.* 1801 . 80, 85, 87, 114, 132, 164, 250, 281

PALGRAVE, FRANCIS TURNER, *b,* 1824 .. 123, 151, 205
PATMORE, COVENTRY, *b.* 1823 . . 94, 134, 136, 182, 186
PROCTER, ADELAIDE ANNE (1825—1864) . 189, 203, 234

ROSCOE, WILLIAM CALDWELL (1823—1857) . 155, 174, 184, 199, 277, 279, 280
ROSSETTI, CHRISTINA, *b.* 1827 . . . 49, 58, 231, 255
ROSSETTI, DANTE GABRIEL, *b.* 1828 48, 51, 114, 174, 215, 220

SCOTT, WILLIAM BELL, *b.* 1812 . 55, 56, 150, 161, 284
SIDNEY, SIR PHILIP (1554—1586) 188, 253
SMEDLEY, MENELLA BUTE, *pub.* 1868 . . . 172
SUTTON, HENRY SEPTIMUS, *pub.* 1854 . 109, 111, 128

TENNYSON, ALFRED, *b.* 1809 . . 144, 162, 252, 287, 288, 290
TENNYSON, FREDERICK, *pub.* 1854 . . . 4, 44, 46
THOREAU, HENRY D. (1817—1862) 230
TOWNSHEND, CHAUNCY HARE (1800—1868) . . 91
TRENCH, RICHARD CHENEVIX, *b.* 1807 . 127, 176, 201
TURNER, CHARLES (TENNYSON), *pub.* 1830, 1868 5, 6, 151, 167, 260

VAUGHAN, HENRY (1621—1695) . . 60, 88, 118, 131, 158, 196, 236, 247, 249, 275

WHITE, JOSEPH BLANCO (1775—1841) . . . 256
WHITNEY, ADELINE D. TRAIN., *b.* 1824 . . . 270
WHITTIER, JOHN GREENLEAF, *b.* 1808 . . 141, 266
WILLIAMS, SARAH, *d.* 1868 . . . . 95, 104, 136
WILSON, JOHN (1785—1854) 63
WORDSWORTH, WILLIAM (1770—1850) 3, 8, 13, 16, 20, 21, 28, 39, 41, 42, 67, 73, 130, 204, 237, 257

ANONYMOUS.

	PAGE
FROM ADELA CATHCART, 1864	97
HYMNS FOR CHR. CHURCH AND HOME, 1840	163
NIGHTINGALE VALLEY, 1862	19
SONGS OF TWO WORLDS, 1871	79

INDEX OF FIRST LINES.

PAGE

A cloud lay cradled near the setting sun 63
A figure wanders through my dreams 172
Ah! bitter chance, no arm the blow could ward . . 260
A little child lay on its mother's knee 46
A little low-ceiled room. Four walls 270
All are not taken: there are left behind 277
All blessings ask a blessed mood 136
A messenger that stood beside my bed 101
And whither, O ye vapours, do ye wend . . ' . . 54
An idle poet here and there 186
Another hand is beckoning us 266
Art thou already weary of the way? 96
As, one dark morn, I trod a forest glade 6
As on my bed at dawn I mused and prayed . . . 5
As ships becalmed at eve that lay 213
As Time one day by me did pass 249
As Winter in some mild autumnal days 184
At early morn I watched, scarce consciously . . . 56
At me, one night, the angry moon 112
At noontide came a voice, Thou must away . . . 232
A wanderer is man, from his birth 225

Beautiful Evelyn Hope is dead 264
Because I knew not when my life was good . . . 104
Be not afraid to pray; to pray is right 123

PAGE

Be, rather than be called, a child of God 261
Blaspheme not thou thy sacred life, nor turn   .   .   . 168
But to be still! oh, but to cease awhile   222

Comes something down with eventide   9
Consider the sea's listless chime   51
Courage of heart and hand, Faith first of all   .   .   . 161

Darkling, methinks, the path of life is grown   .   .   . 229
Day after day, until to-day   94
Dear and great angel, wouldst thou only leave .   .   . 199
Dear friend, far off, my lost desire 287
Dear night, this world's defeat 196
Death, be not proud, though some have called thee .   . 254
Death was full urgent with thee, sister dear   .   .   . 250
Die down, O dismal day, and let me live 54
Die to thy root, sweet flower 56
Dim shadows gather thickly round 234
Does the road wind up-hill all the way? 231
Dreaming, I slept.   Three crosses stood 97
Drop, drop, slow tear   116

Each day a page is of my being's book   109
Ethereal minstrel! pilgrim of the sky   41

Fain would my thoughts fly up to Thee 117
Fair daffodils, we weep to see 52
Fair leaf so crisped and curled and yet so fair .   .   . 59
Fear death, to feel the fog in my throat 233
Fever and fret and aimless stir 153
Five years have passed, five summers, with the length .   21
Follow me, Jesus said, and they uprose 150
From low to high doth dissolution climb 204

PAGE

Give me thy joy in sorrow, gracious Lord	91
Give pardon, blessed soul, to my bold cries	254
Glad sight, wherever new with old	28
Go thou into thy closet, shut thy door	92
Grieve not much for loss of wealth	110
Had this effulgence disappeared	16
Happy those early days when I	236
Here by the sunless lake there is no air	53
Here in this paradise of light	43
How didst thou start, thou holy Baptist, bid	85
How fresh, O Lord, how sweet and clean	156
How often and how vainly do we try	55
How pure at heart and sound in head	288
How soon hath Time, the subtle thief of youth	72
How sweet it were if, without feeble fright	183
How the blithe lark runs up the golden stair	44
I cannot mount to heaven beneath this ban	167
I cannot think that thou shouldst pass away	271
I classed, appraising once	177
I count the dismal time by months and years	219
I do not ask, O Lord, that life may be	203
If fate Love's dear ambition mar	182
If only once the chariot of the morn	4
If we with earnest effort could succeed	127
I got me flowers to strew thy way	134
I grieve not that ripe knowledge takes away	28
I have been in the meadows all the day	207
I heard a thousand blended notes	13
I mourn no more my vanished years	141
In this dim world of clouding cares	262
In trouble for my sin I cried to God	103
I plucked a honeysuckle where	48
I said the darkness shall content my soul	136

PAGE

I saw two children hushed to death 257
I say to thee, do thou repeat 176
Is not the body more than meat, the soul . . . 160
I sought you, friends of youth, in sun and shade . . 222
I struck the board and cried, No more 90
It chanced upon the merry, merry Christmas eve . . 82
It fortifies my soul to know 145
I think this is the very stillest place 53
I thought to meet no more, so dreary seemed . . . 272
It is a beauteous evening, calm and free 20
It is not growing like a tree 78
I walked the other day to spend my hour . . . 158
I wandered lonely as a cloud. 8
I watched a rosebud very long 49
I wished that when you died last May 284
I worship Thee, sweet will of God 148

Joy for the promise of our loftier homes 220
Joy of my life while left me here 275

Knows he who tills this lonely field 281

Lead, kindly Light, amid the encircling gloom . . 164
Leave me, O Love which reachest but to dust . . . 188
Lessons sweet of Spring returning 36
Let me not deem that I was made in vain . . . 74
Let us not teach and preach so much 83
Life and thought have gone away 252
Life, I know not what thou art 231
Light flows our war of mocking words, and yet . . 208
Like morning or the early buds in Spring . . . 199
Like one pale, flitting, lonely gleam 171
Little thinks in the field yon red-cloaked clown . . 14
Live all thy sweet life through 58
Look in my face ; my name is Might-have-been . . 215
Lord, in this dust thy sovereign voice 132

PAGE

Lord, what a change within us one short hour . . . 127
Lord, what am I that with unceasing care . . . 112
Lord, with what care hast Thou begirt us round . . 106
Lord, with what courage and delight 131
Love in thy heart like living waters rose 184
Love is the star by which our course we steer . . . 180

Man dwells apart, though not alone 99
Methinks we do as fretful children do 289
Milton, thou shouldst be living at this hour . . . 73
Mortal, if e'er thy spirits faint 114
Most sweet it is with unuplifted eyes 3
Mountain gorses, ever golden 29
Mourner, that dost deserve thy mournfulness . . ⁓ 97
My God, I heard this day 11
My heart is full of inarticulate pain 197
My heart leaps up when I behold 16
My life is like a stroll upon the beach 230
My little doves have left a nest 30
Mysterious night, when our first parent knew . . . 256

Nature's least worthy growths have quickest spring . . 155

Of all the thoughts of God that are 190
O Father, I have sinned ! I have done 111
O for the happy days gone by 119
Of this fair volume which we World do name . . . 27
O God, impart thy blessing to my cries 151
O God, I thank Thee for a homely taste 135
O happy days, O months, O years 201
Oh yet we trust that somehow good 162
O it is hard to work for God 69
O Lord, my heart is sick 124
O living will that shalt endure 290
One feast, of holy days the crest 77

PAGE

One lesson, Nature, let me learn of thee 40
One month is passed, another is begun 57
One who was suffering tumult in his soul 39
O only Source of all our light and life 129
O sing, clear brook, sing on, while, in a dream . . 218
O Thou of purer eyes than to behold 106
O Thou who, as our knowledge grows 123
Our love is not a fading, earthly flower 182

Prune thou thy words, the thoughts control . . . 80
Put forth thy leaf, thou lofty plane 166

River that stealest with such silent pace 276

Sad soul, whom God, resuming what He gave . . . 279
Say not the struggle nought availeth 167
See how the orient dew 61
Since Nature's works be good, and death doth serve . 253
She sat and wept beside his feet ; the weight . . . 115
Some future day, when what is now is not . . . 170
Soul of my friend, if in thy heavenly rest 272
Speak low to me, my Saviour, low and sweet . . . 202
Stern daughter of the voice of God 67
Still young and fine ! but what is still in view . . . 60
Strong Son of God, immortal love 144
Surprised by joy, impatient as the wind 257
Sweet day, so cool, so calm, so bright 62
Sweet maiden, for so calm a life 258

Take them, O Death, and bear away 289
That music breathes all through my spirit . . . 137
The lights o'er yonder snowy range 64
The lost days of my life until to-day 114
The morning mist is cleared away 35
The mother will not turn who thinks she hears . . 220
The prayers I make will then be sweet indeed . . . 130

PAGE

There is a garden where lilies 205
There is an awful quiet in the air 122
There's not a nook within this solemn Pass . . . 42
There was a gathered stillness in the room . . . 284
There was a time when meadow, grove, and stream . . 237
The sea awoke at midnight from its sleep 42
The starry skies, they rest my soul 192
The sweetest blossoms die 255
The westering sun in copious floods 277
The wind sounds only in opposing straits . . . 101
The woman singeth at her spinning-wheel . . . 81
They are all gone into the world of light 247
They bid me sing to thee 215
The year lies dying in this evening light 19
They say that God lives very high 147
This world is all too sad for tears 95
Thought is deeper than all speech 180
Thou say'st, Take up thy cross 151
Thou who dost dwell alone 107
Three worlds there are, the first of sense 7
Thrice happy he whose name is writ above . . . 71
Thy way is in the deep, O Lord 163
Time was I shrank from what was right 85
'Tis far away, dear friend, 'tis far away 223
'Twas so ; I saw thy birth. That drowsy lake . . 118
Two years ago, this day, he died 285
Type of celestial labour, toil divine 39

Verse, a breeze 'mid blossoms straying 205

Weary of myself and sick of asking 74
We asked not to be born ; 'tis not by will . . . 161
We ask for peace, O God 189
We cannot kindle when we will 76
Weep not for me 281

	PAGE
Weighing the steadfastness and state	88
We overstate the ills of life, and take	100
We sat within the farmhouse old	211
We watched her breathing through the night	269
What is it that is gone, we fancied ours?	50
What mean these slow returns of love, these days	128
What's that which ere I spake was gone?	134
What were I, love, if I were stripped of thee	187
What we, when face to face we see	169
What wonder man should fail to stay	185
Whence thou hast come thou knowest not, little brook	217
When God at first made man	89
When I consider how my light is spent	72
When I look back upon my former race	87
When the enemy is near thee	146
When vain desire at last and vain regret	174
When we were idlers with the loitering rills	186
Where lies the land to which the ship would go?	228
White-throated swans and sedges of the mere	218
Whither, 'midst falling dew	33
Who feels not when the Spring once more	6
Who, toiling on the weary round of life	79
Who will say the world is dying	165
Why fear that the departed grieves	280
With her white hands claspt she sleepeth	261
Yellow leaves on the ash-tree	174
Ye who would build the churches of the Lord	147

GILBERT AND RIVINGTON, LIMITED, ST. JOHN'S SQUARE, LONDON.